SWISS RAILWAYS

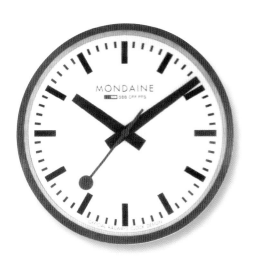

The standard official SBB/CFF/FFS station clock;
timekeeping on Swiss railways is always
of paramount importance.

SWISS RAILWAYS

SIX DECADES OF CHANGE

PHILIP J. KELLEY

SHREW
DALE
PUBLISHING

THE AUTHOR

Born in Guernsey, Channel Islands, in 1928, Philip J. Kelley first came to the mainland permanently in 1936 and was immediately drawn to railways, encouraged, no doubt, by his late Father who was also an enthusiast. He was married in 1964 but now a widower after his wife died in 2007.

He was employed by British Railways from 1948 to 1988 and, during his railway career, has served as a photographer and has worked in both the BTC Archives and the Museum at Clapham. His final position was as Historical Buildings Assistant to the Chief Architect British Railways Board. After retirement from BR, he worked for the NHS until reaching 65. He has travelled extensively throughout Europe, especially Switzerland, Scandinavia and Zimbabwe. He is still, at 85, a keen photographer of prototype railways and model railways, and possesses a 'O' gauge layout in his garden. He is the author of books concerning GWR road vehicles as well as an earlier short book on Swiss Mountain Railways, which was published in 1999.

He is a Trustee of the Great Western Trust at Didcot Railway Centre, where he is instrumental, with others, in providing displays in the Museum & Archive building. He is also a member of many other railway and model railway societies, including the Swiss Railway Society.

Other interests include being a member of the Royal Observer Corps, which was stood down in the 1990s, and a Church Organist.

Dedicated to John Goodman, my very good friend and Swiss enthusiast.

SWISS RAILWAYS
Philip J. Kelley
First published 2014

ISBN 978 0 9575898 1 0

Book design: Mark Nelson

All photographs were taken by the author or are from his collection unless otherwise credited.

Published by the author through Shrewdale Publishing, 25 Monkmoor Road, Shrewsbury, SY2 5AG

Distributed by Bookworld, Unit 10, Hodfar Road, Sandy Lane Industrial Estate, Stourport, DY13 9QB

Printed in China

CONTENTS

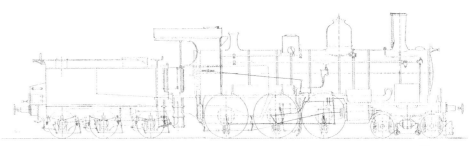

Abbildung 88.   B B

ACKNOWLEDGEMENTS

I AM very grateful for the very generous help that the Swiss Federal Railways, the Swiss Locomotive Works and all the other railways in Switzerland have given me over the years. This includes all the time that members of their operating and outside staff have assisted me without hesitation. It is very much appreciated. Thanks also go to many friends and relations residing in Switzerland. I should especially like to thank John Goodman, Charles Vier, Brian Clark, Donald Binns, Alan Pike, Brian Hemming and others for their help in providing information and photographs. My very grateful thanks also go to Mrs Ute Lord who has helped me considerably with the very difficult technical German translations. There are many more friends who are unfortunately no longer with us but have given me a lot of help in the past, particularly Henry Ernst, Cecil J. Allen, Ian Duncan and C. R. Gordon Stuart.

I would also like to thank Peter Waller for all his encouragement in the compilation of this book and his help in getting it published and Mark Nelson for his excellent design.

The photographs in this book are mostly taken by the author or come from his collection; where this is not the case, they are credited to the individuals or companies concerned. A number of the photographs, drawings, postcards, plans, etc used have come from a variety of sources and every effort has been made to obtain permission where required. If I have overlooked anything, or unwittingly infringed anyone's copyright, I offer my sincere apologies.

Philip J. Kelley,
Wiltshire,
July 2013

GERMAN-ENGLISH RAILWAY NOMENCLATURE

Amtliches Kursbuch	Official timetable
Bahnhof	Station
Bahnsteig	Platform
Bundesbahn	Federal railway
Dampflok	Steam locomotive
Diesellok	Diesel locomotive
Drahtseilbahn	Funicular
Eisenbahn	Railway
Electrolok	Electric locomotive
Gepäcktriebwagen	Luggage van
Gleis	Track
Güterzug	Freight train
Hauptbahnhof	Main station
Höchstgeschwindigkeit	Top speed
Luftseilbahn	Cableway
Normalspur	Standard gauge
Personenwagen	Passenger coach
Personenzug	Slow or stopping train
Personen und Güterzug	Mixed train
Schlepptender	Tender
Schmalspur	Narrow gauge
Schnellzug	Fast train (Express)
Strassenbahn	Tramway
Triebwagen	Railcar
Zahnradbahn	Rack railway
Zug	Train

ABBREVIATIONS

ABB	ASEA Brown Boveri, Baden
AEG	Allgemeine Elecktizitätsgesellschaft, Berlin
BBC	AG Brown Boveri & Cie, Baden
CFF	Chemins de Fer Fédéraux
FFS	Ferrovie Federali Svizzera
MAN	Maschinenfabrik Augsburg Nürnberg AG, Germany
MFO	Maschinenfabrik Oerlikon, Zürich
SAAS	Société Anonyme des Ateliers de Sécheron, Geneva
SBB	Schweizerische Bundesbahnen
SIG	Schweizerische Industrie Gesellschaft, Neuhausen am Rheinfall
SLM	Schweizerische Lokomotiv und Maschinen fabrik, Winterthur
SOB	Schweizerische Südostbahn
SWP	Schindler Waggon AG, Pratteln,
SWS	Schweizerische Wagons und Aufzügefabrik AG, Schlieren

Most railway company names and initials are shown throughout the book.

INTRODUCTION

THE main idea behind this book is to show by means of photographs — the majority of which are in colour — the variety of Switzerland's transport systems over the years. Most of the photographs, taken by the author, date from the early 1950s, 1967 and lastly 2008. Black and white pictures are also included because of their historical interest, as well as quite a selection of old postcards from my large collection.

The Swiss realised right from the start that their scenery was superb and it was very important to enable their own people and later tourists to be able to travel extensively. Even today it is recognised that it is vitally important that communication by rail, especially in the winter months, is maintained. The technical achievement in getting some of these lines to the summits of mountains is really incredible. Various gauges were used — standard (1,435mm), metre, and 800mm — depending on the type of terrain to be covered. Some lines are adhesion only, rack and adhesion, and rack only. There are other systems, of course; namely funiculars, cable cars and chair lifts, etc.

Much has been written about the history of Swiss Railways so I will not go into a lot of detail but only quote salient points. The first purely Swiss line was opened on 9 August 1847 between Zürich and Baden. (In the author's extensive library of books dealing with Swiss subjects three different dates are given for this opening: 7, 8 and 9 August. I have chosen the 9th, as that appears to be the date the line was opened to the public.) Further lines were opened over the years, as in Britain. In 1850, the Swiss Government asked Robert Stephenson to advise on a comprehensive railway system that would link the major cities of the country.

Eventually, most of the Stephenson lines were built and constituted the nucleus of the Swiss system; these were all privately constructed to the standard gauge. The North Eastern Railway was formed on 1 July

Poster advertising the opening of Switzerland's first railway line — from Zürich to Baden — on 1 May 1847. Although services by the Schweizerische Nord Bahn (Swiss Northern Railway) were supposed to start on that date, delays meant that the first trains did not operate until 9 August 1847. The timetable suggested that the journey time would be 30min for the 23.3km (14.5 miles) but this proved impractical and in reality the trains took some 45min.

Continued on page xiv.

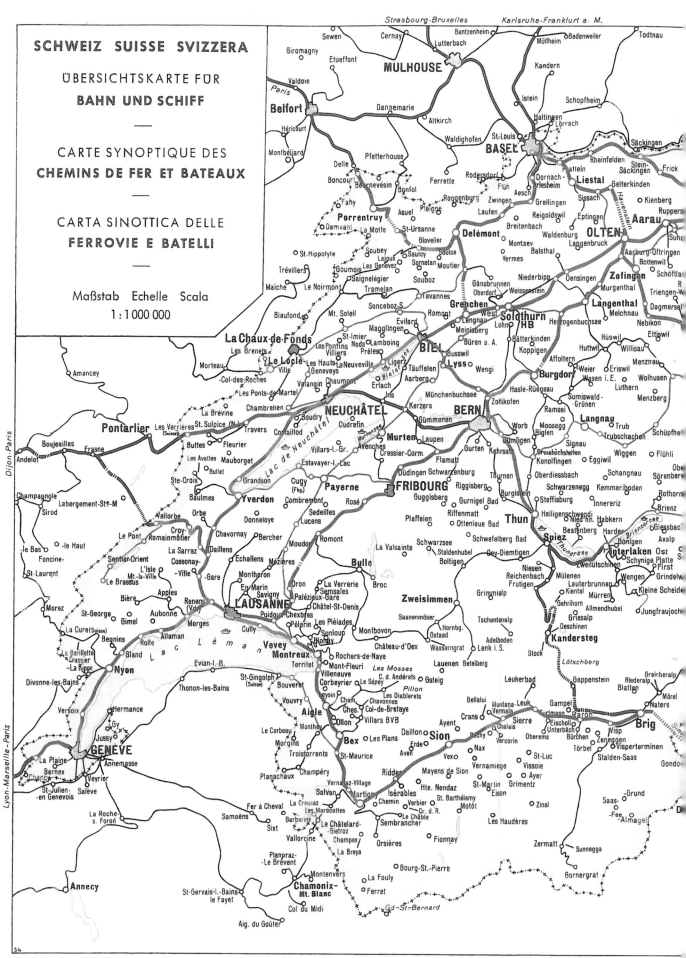

Map of Switzerland and its railways in 1954. Kümmerley & Frey

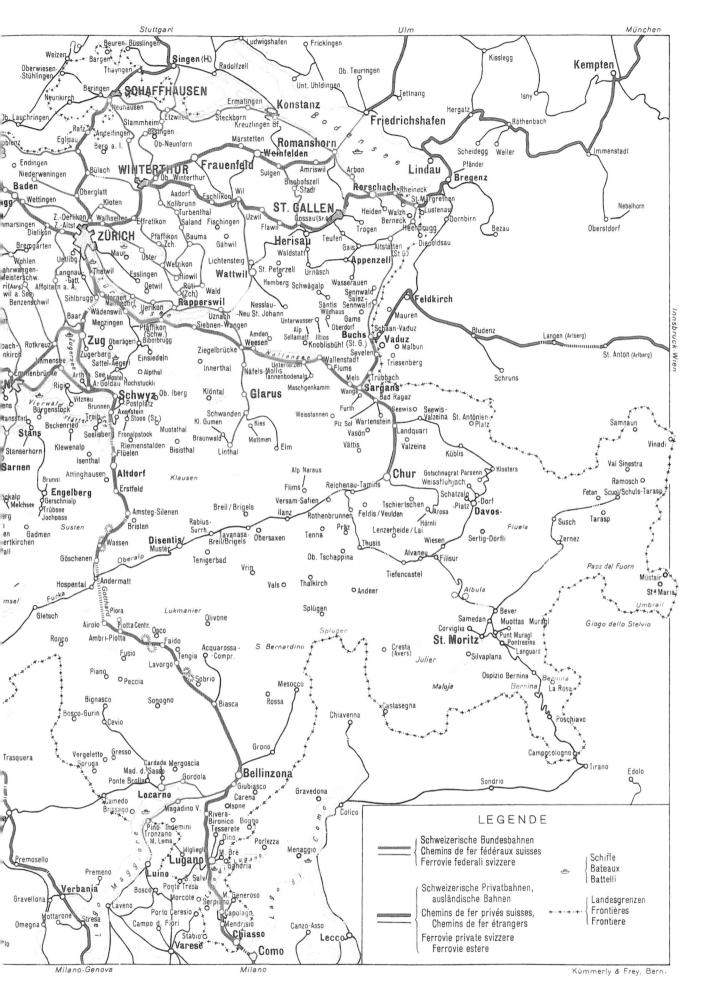

LEGENDE

Schweizerische Bundesbahnen
Chemins de fer fédéraux suisses
Ferrovie federali svizzere

Schiffe
Bateaux
Battelli

Schweizerische Privatbahnen,
ausländische Bahnen
Chemins de fer privés suisses,
Chemins de fer étrangers
Ferrovie private svizzere
Ferrovie estere

Landesgrenzen
Frontières
Frontiere

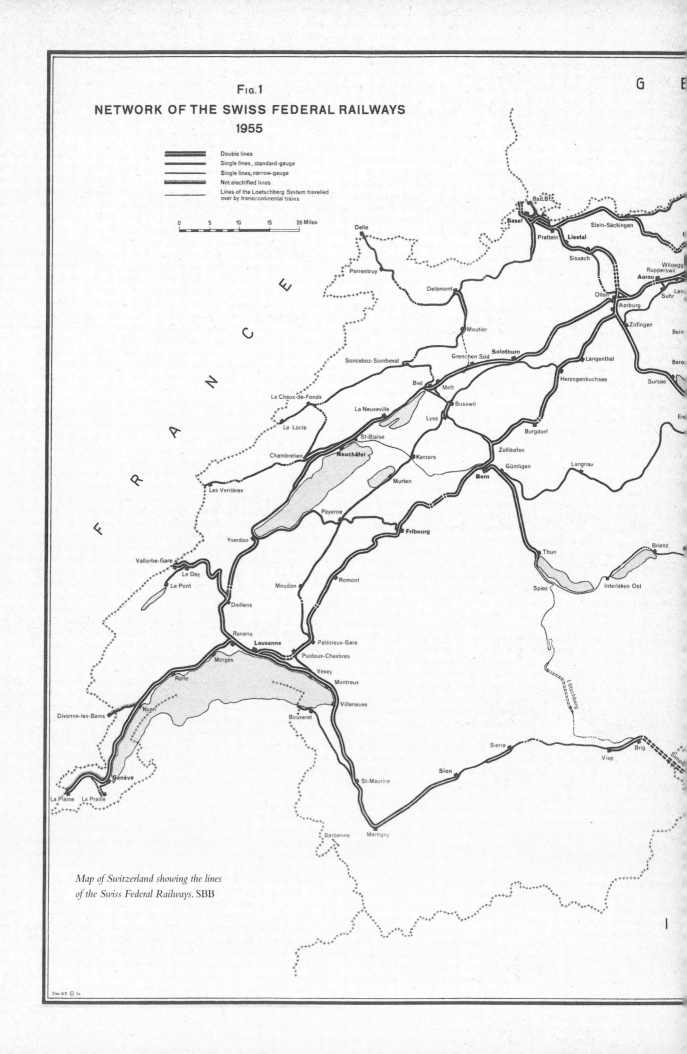

Map of Switzerland showing the lines
of the Swiss Federal Railways. SBB

x

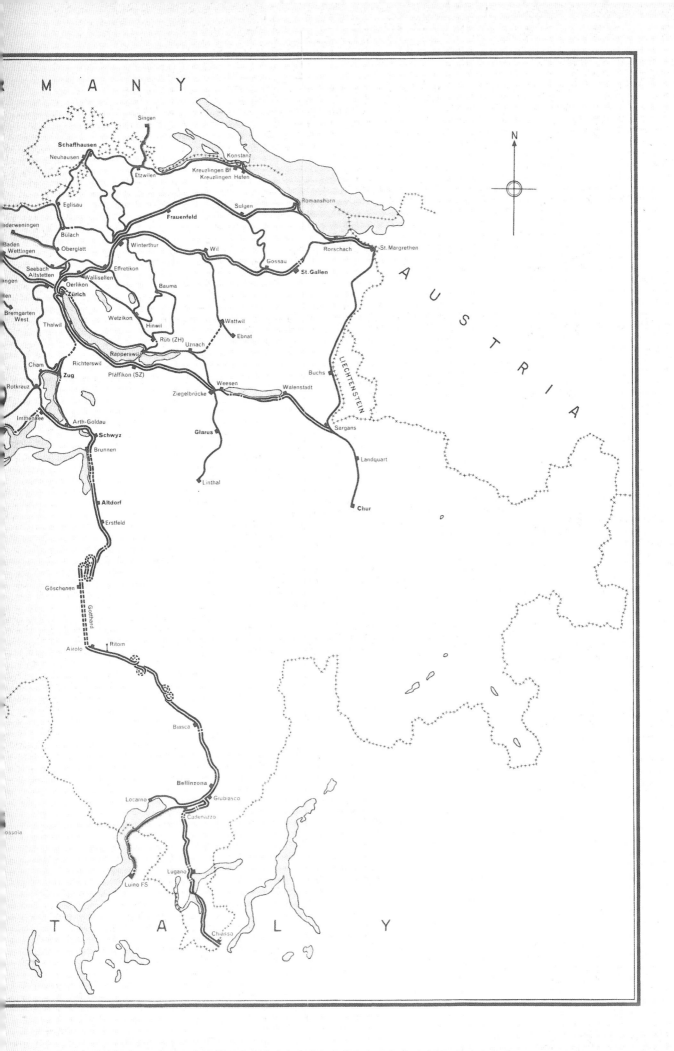

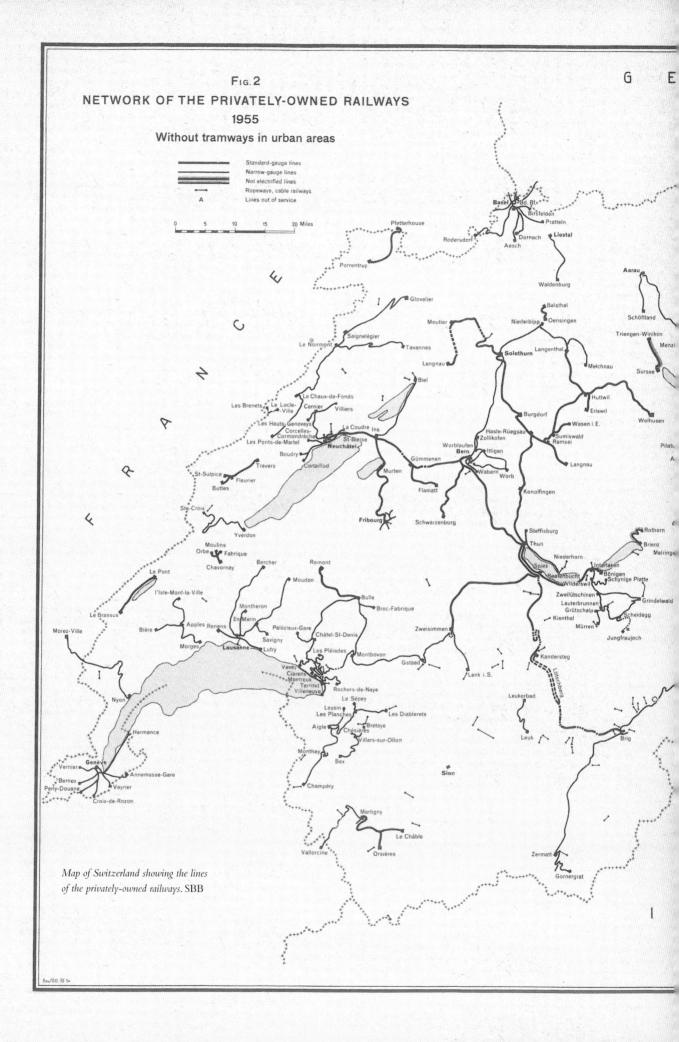

FIG. 2

NETWORK OF THE PRIVATELY-OWNED RAILWAYS
1955
Without tramways in urban areas

Standard-gauge lines
Narrow-gauge lines
Not electrified lines
Ropeways, cable railways
Lines out of service

0   5   10   15   20 Miles

Map of Switzerland showing the lines
of the privately-owned railways. SBB

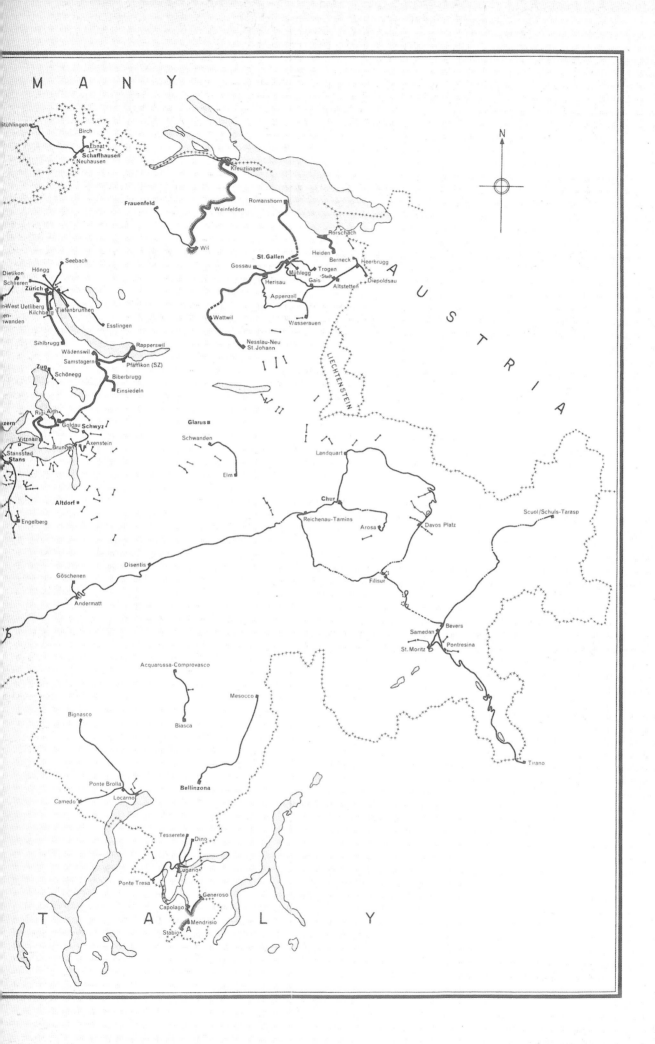

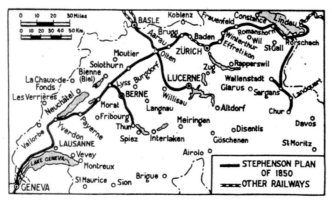

A map illustrating the lines proposed by Robert Stephenson in 1850.
Railway Gazette

1853, the Central Railway was formed on 26 August 1852, the United Swiss Railways system was incorporated on 6 January 1853, the Gotthard Railway was formed on 1 November 1871, and the Western Swiss and Jura Lines also came into the picture. These five mainline companies were eventually nationalised to become the Swiss Federal Railways (SBB/CFF/FFS) on 1 January 1902. However, other standard-gauge lines remained private such as the Lötschberg (BLS), the South Eastern Railway, etc.

The only metre-gauge line to become part of the Swiss Federal Railway system is the Brünig line, which runs between Luzern and Interlaken; this is now known as the Zentralbahn and is not the responsibility of SBB.

Switzerland is often referred to as the 'turntable of Europe' because of the international routes that run through the country and the alpine tunnels. A map showing these appears in the section on the Gotthard line on page 1. New tunnels are now being planned or undertaken, known as 'base' tunnels, in order to avoid the approach spiral tunnels and thus speed up journey times. One such is the Lötschberg that opened on 15 June 2007.

The first steam locomotive to operate in Switzerland was the Schweizerische Nord Bahn's 4-2-0 Limmat, *which was one of two supplied by the Karlsruhe Works of Emil Kessler for the opening of the line in 1847. The original locomotive was withdrawn in 1882, following a rebuild in 1866, but a working replica was constructed by SLM (Works No 3937) in 1947 to mark the centenary of Swiss railway operation. The replica was subsequently preserved as part of the collection of the Luzern-based Swiss Institute of Transport.* J. Kündig, Zug & Verkershaus der Schweiz

At 2.30pm on 15 October 2010 the world's longest tunnel made a breakthrough. This new Gotthard base tunnel, known as the New Alpine Transversal (NEAT), is 57km (35.4 miles) in length and has been 17 years in the making. It is due to open in 2017, when it will cut journey times between Zürich and Milan from 3hr 40min to 2hr 50min. Apparently, the deviation on the drilling midway in the tunnel was just 8cm horizontally and 1cm vertically.

Whilst all the standard-gauge lines were being formed and constructed many narrow-gauge lines, both metre and 800mm, were being surveyed and built, including adhesion, rack and adhesion, and rack only. (In Switzerland there are five different types of rack in use — see Appendices for drawings and descriptions.) The construction of rack lines is expensive, so more and more cable car systems are being constructed to gain access to mountain peaks.

The Swiss Government is very proud of its transport, particularly the railways, and gives generous financial support. It was decided about the time of nationalisation (1902) that electrification of the system should be commenced, as there was no indigenous coal in Switzerland and the continued use of steam locomotives was dependent on the import of coal from other countries. This was an unnecessary cost when there were many rivers, lakes and waterfalls in the country that could be adapted to generate hydroelectricity. Over the years from 1902 to 1960, the electrification of the Swiss Federal Railway system was 99.1% complete.

After experiments with different voltages it was decided to standardise on an overhead catenary system using single-phase current at 15kV, 16.7Hz ac. Other private railways, both standard-gauge and narrow-gauge, also gradually converted to electric traction. Many of these companies have their own hydro electric power stations and use current at a variety of voltages. There are one or two which are still steam operated, such as the Brienz Rothorn-Bahn and other preserved lines.

At the time of writing there have been a number of amalgamations of lines and companies, and where applicable these will be dealt with under the lines concerned. Further detailed information will be given with each photograph, drawing or map in the following pages. I have decided to arrange the book in areas showing standard gauge, narrow gauge and other types, but not every line in Switzerland is covered, the main focus being on the most popular tourist areas.

Many railways throughout Switzerland have received or are receiving new locomotives and rolling stock, some but not all of which are shown in this book, as other books and magazines published recently give this information. The main idea behind this book is to show the changes that have taken place over the past 60 years or so. In Switzerland the railways are always developing and improving; it is, therefore, almost impossible to keep up to date. If you would like further information on developments, then I recommend that you join the Swiss Railways Society.

Regarding classification, building dates and Works numbers, the details have mostly been read from the vehicles themselves when they were photographed. Other information has been abstracted from official company records, but even then there is conflicting data. Many vehicles have been reclassified or rebuilt since the photographs were taken; I have, in most cases, quoted the original numbers and details.

THE GOTTHARD LINE
AND ITS ENVIRONS

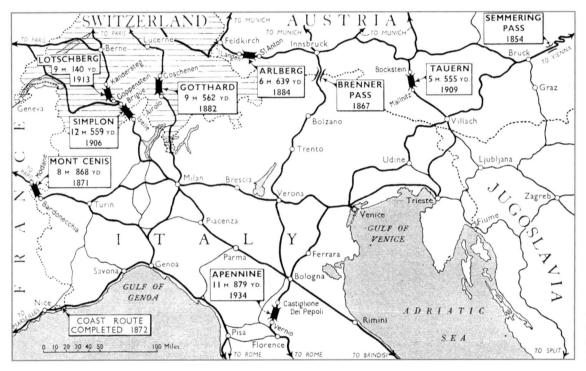

Map showing the location of the alpine tunnels in Switzerland circa 1947.
Railway Gazette

THERE are many routes leading to the Gotthard line, including those from Basel, Olten, Luzern, Zürich plus many others. The Gotthard Railway, its approach lines and its associated tunnel opened throughout on 1 June 1882. The tunnel itself is 14.92km (9 miles 562yd) long and at its centre point is 1,154m (3,786ft) above sea level. The original link with other lines in Switzerland was made at Immensee and connecting lines from Luzern to Immensee and from Zug to Arth-Goldau were not opened until 1 June 1897. The founder of this successful enterprise was Dr Alfred Escher of Zürich, whose statue is outside Zürich Hauptbahnhof. The actual tunnel is between Göschenen in the north and Airolo in the south. Chiasso is where the line leaves Switzerland and enters Italy. I will deal with the line starting at Zürich and show photographs etc travelling southwards.

Between 1956 and 1962, the author worked in the British Transport Commission Archives at 66 Porchester Road near Paddington. I had been travelling to Switzerland many times since 1954, and was giving lectures about Switzerland and its railways in London and elsewhere. At one of my talks,

Henry Ernst, Manager of the Swiss National Tourist Office, made himself known to me. He and the SBB offered me many facilities on the railway system. One such trip was travelling in the cab of a locomotive from Zürich to Lugano on 6 June 1958, and I also spent a week at the signalling school at Zug. This involved travel out and about on the system in cabs and on special railcars.

One of the trips with the signalling school was in a *Roter Pfeil* (Red Arrow) railcar from Zug to Lugano. During the journey the train vigilance system was tested. The driver left the cab with a signal having been set to danger and we gradually came to a stand very gently. This was demonstrated whilst listening to music on a record player and the stylus did not miss a track! We stopped off at Göschenen to observe the 'Motorail' service through the tunnel. A tour was also arranged round Bellinzona railway works.

At Zug there was a metre-gauge *Strassenbahn* (tramway), which ran from the town to Schönegg where it connected with a *Drahtseilbahn* (funicular) to the Zugerberg. The 3km tramway, known as the Zug-Schönegg-Zugerberg, opened on 20 March 1907 and closed on 11 May 1959.

Continued on page 15

The statue of Dr Alfred Escher (1819–1882) outside Zürich Hauptbahnhof in June 1958. He appeared to have died in the year of completion of the tunnel. There is a parallel here with I. K. Brunel, who died in the year of the opening of the Royal Albert Bridge at Saltash.

Above: The meeting of the workmen midway through the St Gotthard Tunnel as recorded by The Illustrated London News *of 13 March 1880 in an issue marking the completion of the tunnel. Author's collection*

The same issue of The Illustrated London News *portrayed the arrival at Airolo of the first train to come through the tunnel. Author's collection*

SBB Triebwagen CFe4/4 No 845, built by SLM in 1952, brings a train into Zürich Hauptbahnhof on 16 June 1956. These locomotives had a driving cab at both ends and were fitted for push-pull working. They were subsequently renumbered into the 1621-51 series and reclassified in 1962 to BDe4/4.

Above: Between Basel and Luzern lies Olten Hauptbahnhof, 39km (24 miles) from Basel and 57km (35 miles) from Luzern, shown here on 25 May 1954. A very busy station, it could almost be likened to Clapham Junction. Note the beautiful vitreous enamel signs.

Above: SBB Class Ae4/7 Universalllokomotive No 10943, built by SLM in 1931, hauls the 15.30 personenzug (stopping train) from Zürich to Chur at Thalwil on 10 June 1956. The line to Sargans and thence to Austria leaves from here.

Zug station: Elektrisches Tasten-Befehlwerk (electric keyboard command desk). SBB

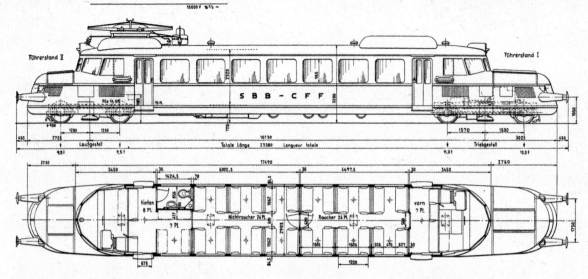

Schweizerische Bundesbahnen
Zugförderungs- und Werkstättedienst

RBe ²/₄ 1008, 1009

Führerstand II   Führerstand I

A drawing shows classification as RBe2/4. SBB.

S B B - C F F

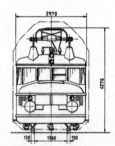

Die RBe 2/4 Nr. 1008 und 1009 (Umbau)

301 Plan mit den technischen Daten der umgebauten CLm 2/4 Nr. 101–102 aus dem Jahre 1935, die als Diesel-Leichttriebwagen zu den SBB kamen. In der SBB-Werkstätte Zürich wurden die zwei Fahrzeuge 1951–53 für den elektrischen Betrieb umgebaut und modernisiert. Doch schon 1964 wurden sie ausgemustert. Noch während der Expo 1964 in Lausanne kamen sie am alten Hauenstein zum Einsatz.

Folgende Seite: **302/302a** Oben und Mitte: Die beiden Seiten des RCe 2/4 Nr. 611 im Werkstätteareal Zürich nach dem Umbau, Februar 1951.

303 Unten: Später wurden die zwei Triebwagen auf RBe 2/4 Nr. 611 und 612 umbezeichnet. Erkennungsmerkmale sind die Deckel auf den Vorbauten und Kasten der Dachwiderstände. Aufnahme in Bellinzona 1959 (Photos SBB).

Trieb- bzw. Laufraddurchmesser		900 mm
Anzahl Fahrmotoren		2
Min. Reibungsgewicht		21 t
Dienstgewicht		40 t
Max. Gewicht (voll belastet)		47 t
Anzahl Sitzplätze		70
Anzahl Stehplätze	ca.	30
Getriebe*)-Übersetzung	1 : 3,38	1 : 2,28
Max. Anfahrzugkraft am Rad	3200 kg	2160 kg
Stundenzugkraft am Rad	1800 kg	1210 kg
Stundenleistung am Rad	327 PS	
Stundenleistung an der Welle	260 kW	
bei V =	49 km/h	73 km/h
Dauerleistung am Rad	257 PS	
Dauerleistung an der Welle	204 kW	
bei V =	60 km/h	89 km/h
Maximale Geschwindigkeit	75 km/h	110 km/h

Elektr. Widerstandsbremse wirkend auf Triebgestell
*) nur im Stillstand umschaltbar

SBB Class RBe2/4 No 611, built by SLM in 1935 and later renumbered 1008, pictured at Lugano on 12 June 1958 after the trip with the signalling school.

SBB Class Ae4/6
No 10805, built by SLM
in 1942, is seen at Zug-
Oberwil, 3km south of Zug,
where we stopped
for photography on
6 June 1958.

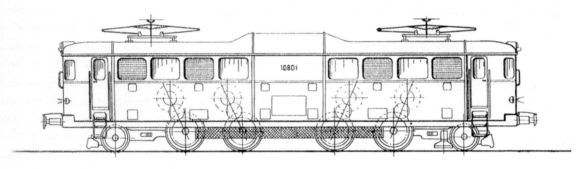

A drawing and technical
details of the SBB
Class Ae4/6.

TS 27   SCHWEIZERISCHE BUNDESBAHNEN   Tafel 35a

Schweizerische Lokomotiv- und Maschinenfabrik / Maschinenfabrik Oerlikon / AG. Brown, Boveri & Cie.
S.A. des Ateliers de Sécheron

Ae 4/6   Nr. 10801–10812   1941–1945   Schnellzugdienst

Spurweite	1435 mm	Max. Anfahrzugkraft am Rad	28000 kg	Fahrdrahtspannung	15000 V
Triebrad-Durchmesser	1350 mm	Stundenzugkraft	17600 kg	Frequenz	$16^{2}/_{3}$ Hz
Laufrad-Durchmesser	950 mm	Geschw'keit b. Stund'zugkraft	85 km/h	Max. Motorspannung	430 V
Übersetzungsverhältnis	1:3,22	Stundenleistung	5540 PS	Länge über Puffer	17260 mm
Dienstgewicht	105 t	Max. Geschwindigkeit	125 km/h	Radstand total	12200 mm
Reibungsgewicht	80 t	Anzahl Triebmotoren	4×2	Universalantrieb Winterthur	

A view of the interior of the führerstand (cab) of an SBB Class Ae4/6.

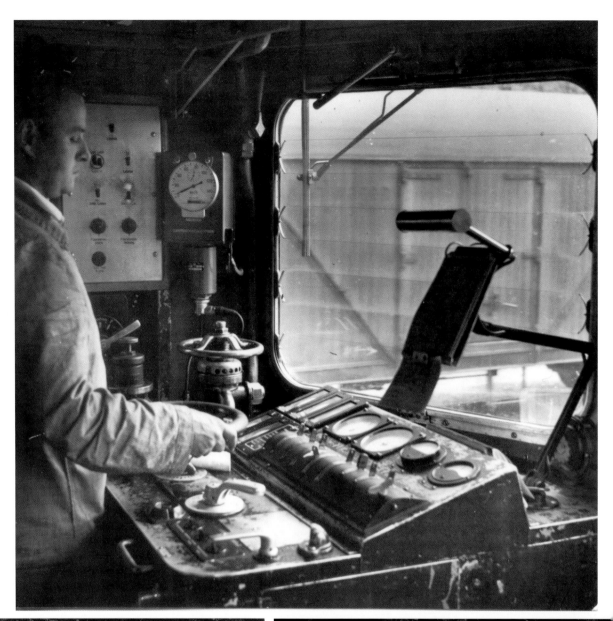

Two views of the Zug Strassenbahn (tramways) with Class Be2/2 Nos 1 (left) and 2 (right).

On 17 June 1958 Class Be2/2 No 3 comes round the Pulverturm ('Powder Tower') in Zug on the Zug Strassenbahn; this building was part of the town's fortifications and presumably must have been the gunpowder store. The vehicles probably date from the beginning of the service and have now been replaced by a bus service.

Above: The lower terminus of the Zug (Schönegg)-Zugerberg funicular at Schönegg on 14 June 1958. It is hard to believe that this chalet-type building is actually a station.

Left: Reproduction of an early postcard promoting the Zug (Schönegg)-Zugerberg Drahtseilbahn (funicular). Biregg Verlag AG, CH-6003, Luzern

The length of the line is 1,275m (4,182ft) and the upper terminus is at 927m (3,042ft). The line is metre gauge and was opened on 14 May 1907. One of the cars is pictured en route to the summit; it is having a repaint.

Zug is noted for its sunsets and it is worth stopping here just for the experience. This was the scene on 17 June 1958.

C. J. Kelley, Esq.,
"Colyton",
16, Broadmead Road,
WOODFORD GREEN,
Essex, England.

Many stations in Switzerland also acted as post offices. The author's late father was a philatelist as well as a railway enthusiast. He specialised in postmarks and, whilst in Switzerland, visited most of the obscure post offices and arranged for samples to be sent home on self-addressed letters. This example came from the Zugerberg.

ZUG
Bahnhof

The landing stage for steamer departures and arrivals near Zug station on the Zugersee, seen on 20 June 1958.

9

Zugersee steamer Rigi, photographed on 20 June 1958. This vessel is not to be confused with the 1847 Rigi that, at the time, was preserved in the Verkehrshaus der Schweiz (Swiss Transport Museum) in Luzern. The places served by the steamer on the Zugersee were Cham, Oberwil, Risch, Walchwil, Immensee and Arth, where a tram connected with Goldau. This tram will be dealt with later in the book.

A model of the typical lake steamer complete with the statutory Swiss flag anchored on the Zugersee on 20 June 1958. The author was unable to find out anything about the model.

The new order on 21 June 1958: a bus and trailer pictured at Zug station on a service to Oberägeri, on the Ägerisee, a distance of 13.6km. The service was run by the Zugerland Verkehrsbetriebe transport company.

SBB Class Ae6/6 No 11401 Ticino, built by SLM in 1952 and the first of the class, was provided for the author's trip from Zürich to Lugano on 6 June 1958 and is shown here at Arth-Goldau. The line from Luzern comes in here. Also the Arth-Rigi-Bahn operates from this point to the summit of the Rigi. This line will be dealt with later.

The interior of a Class Ae6/6 locomotive. SBB

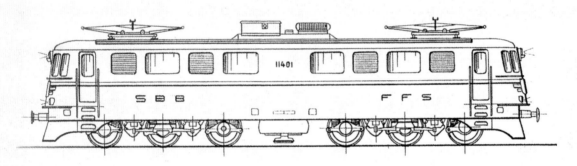

TS 33   SCHWEIZERISCHE BUNDESBAHNEN   Tafel 37c
Schweizerische Lokomotiv- und Maschinenfabrik   *AG. Brown, Boveri & Cie.*
Ae 6/6   Nr. 11401–11402   1952–1953   Schnellzugdienst

Spurweite	1435 mm	Max. Anfahrzugkraft am Rad	33 000 kg	Fahrdrahtspannung	15 000 V
Triebrad-Durchmesser	1260 mm	Stundenzugkraft	21 200 kg	Frequenz	$16^2/_3$ Hz
Laufrad-Durchmesser	—	Geschw'keit b. Stund'zugkraft	75 km/h	Max. Motorspannung	500 V
Übersetzungsverhältnis	1 : 2,216	Stundenleistung	6000 PS	Länge über Puffer	18 400 mm
Dienstgewicht	122,5 t	Max. Geschwindigkeit	125 km/h	Radstand total	13 000 mm
Reibungsgewicht	122,5 t	Anzahl Triebmotoren	6	BBC-Federantrieb	

Drawing and technical dimensions for the SBB Class Ae6/6. SBB

The view ahead from the cab of the Class Ae6/6 shows the beautifully manicured track and the very light overhead structures of the SBB. Left-hand running was the order of the day and reflected the early British influence. Today most lines are signalled for bi-directional running.

SBB Class Ae6/6 No 11418 St Gallen is seen at Arth-Goldau on 16 June 1958. The locomotive was one of a batch built by SLM between 1955 and 1956. The very nice green livery and the front-end embellishment, which the early members of the class carried, show up very well.

As mentioned, there was a tram service from Arth-Goldau station to the town of Arth. Metre gauge four-wheel tram No 2 is shown here at Arth-Goldau on 16 June 1958, complete with post box. The tram was built by Maschinenfabrik Augsberg & Mashinenfabrik Geshellschaft Nürnberg AG in 1905 (Works No 63214). The Swiss did occasionally go to builders outside the country for locomotives and rolling stock.

Below: SOB Triebwagen Class BFe4/4 No 62 at Einsiedeln on 17 June 1958 when it was just ex-Works. It was built by SLM circa 1955; similar vehicles were supplied to the SBB.

At Arth-Goldau there is another railway; this is the Schweizerische Südostbahn (South Eastern Railway). The original line was from Wädenswil to Einsiedeln and opened on 1 May 1877. The Rapperswil to Pfäffikon line was opened on 27 August 1878 as the Zürichsee-Gotthardbahn. The Südostbahn was formed in 1889 to take over the original lines and build a line from Pfäffikon to Samstagern with a connection to Biberbrücke and Arth-Goldau; these opened on 8 August 1891, and were electrified on 15 May 1939. A merger took place in 2002, when the Bodensee-Toggenburg and the Schweizerische Südostbahn became the Südostbahn.

Coming further south on the Gotthard line passengers reach Schwyz, 8km (5 miles) from Arth-Goldau, where, in 1956, there remained a metre-gauge tramway known as the Schwyzer *Strassenbahn*. This ran to Ibach and Brunnen SBB *Bahnhof* and *Schiffstation*. The next station coming south is Flüelen, 12km (8 miles) from Brunnen. Further south we come to the famous spiral tunnels on the north side of the Gotthard Tunnel; these were driven in order to gain height without very steep gradients thus enabling the train to maintain a good speed. Work is in progress to bore base tunnels that will make the tunnels longer, but — being on the level — train speeds will be higher. A similar system exists on the south side of the Gotthard Tunnel. The most famous are those near Wassen.

Following the Gotthard Tunnel, the line now heads to Giubiasco junction for Locarno and Luino (Italy), which is 3km from Bellinzona. From Giubiasco it is only 20km down the branch to Locarno.

At Locarno a metre-gauge line runs to Domodossola in Italy. In 1906, following the opening of the Simplon Tunnel, plans were mooted for a link to the Gotthard line. The resulting metre-gauge Centovalli Railway, as it is also known, became very important. At Ponte Brolla — 9km from

SOB Triebwagen Class Be4/4 No 11, which was built circa 1939, is pictured arriving at Einsiedeln on 17 June 1958. In the author's opinion, these were not the best looking of vehicles.

SOB Elektrische Traktoren Class Te2/2 No 31, built by SLM/SAAS in 1943, shunts four-wheel coaches and a wagon at Einsiedeln on 17 June 1958.

Above: Schwyzer Strassenbahnen No 5 awaits passengers at Brunnen Schiffstation on 13 June 1956. This route was opened on 6 October 1900 and closed on 15 December 1963. The line was 7.09km long and was ac electric from the start. At Brunnen there was a rack railway to Axenstein; this is dealt with in the Luzern section of the book (see page 147).

Einsiedeln is a place of pilgrimage; the monastery building, which dates to 1704-35, is the largest and finest masterpiece of baroque architecture in Switzerland. As a result it generates a considerable amount of traffic for the Südostbahn. This view shows the building on 17 June 1958, with an interesting assortment of cars in the car park.

SBB Class Ae6/6 No 11401 heads a train at Flüelen bound for Luzern on 13 June 1956. A large party of passengers from the buses shown parked in the station forecourt entrained here. Note the footbridge, which is reminiscent of British Midland Railway design.

Göschenen lies at the northern end of the Gotthard Tunnel. This early postcard shows Gotthardbahn Class A3/5 Dampflokomotive No 211 emerging from the tunnel circa 1900. E. Goetz, Luzern/Author's collection

Locarno — a branch line ran up to Bignasco via the Mággia Valley. The branch opened on 2 July 1907, but is now closed, with the journey now taken by bus. The line to Domodossola is 132km (82 miles) long and is jointly owned by the Ferrovie Autolinee Regionali Ticinese (FART) and the Italian Società Subalpina di Imprese Ferroviarie (SSIF).

The scenery on this route is spectacular and the line opened throughout on 27 November 1923 using 1,300V dc with adhesion working only. The frontier between Switzerland and Italy is at Camedo. In 1979/80 the line was very badly damaged by storms.

We now arrive at Lugano, which is 199km (125 miles) from Luzern. At the time of the author's second visit to Lugano in 1958 there were still trams in operation to the base terminus of the Lugano-San Salvatore funicular at Paradiso. The metre-gauge line, which was 4.6km (3 miles) in length,

Map of the spiral tunnels and gradient profile of the Gotthard line.
Railway Gazette

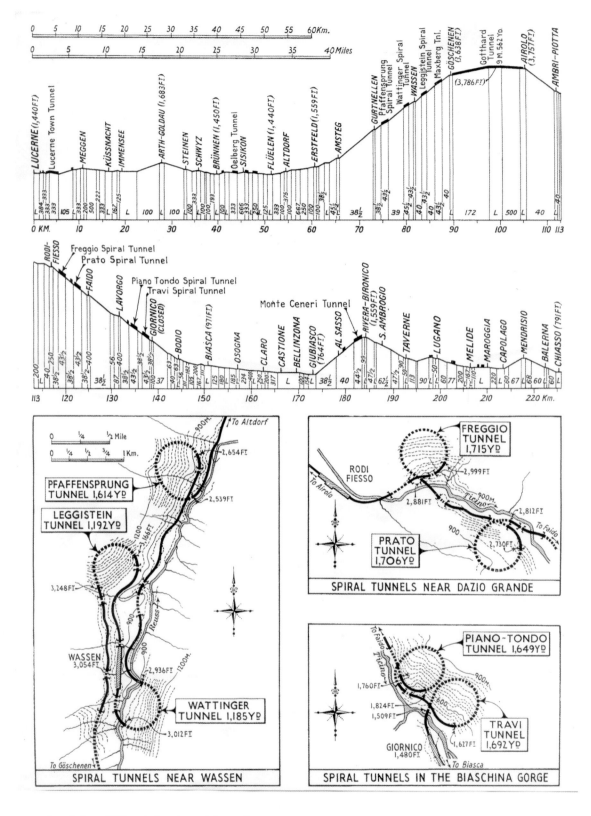

opened on 1 June 1896 and closed on 17 December 1959. The service is now operated by buses.

Six kilometres (4 miles) south of Lugano is the crossing point where the Gotthard line goes over Lake Lugano between Melide and Bissone. Engineers discovered the underwater ridge that was ideal for establishing the formation to carry the line southwards.

At Capolago passengers can join the Ferrovia del Monte Generoso (MG) which is an Abt system, 800mm-gauge rack line. The line opened from Capolago to Bellavista on 5 June 1890 and from Bellavista to the summit at Vetta on 22 June 1890 and is 8.85km (5½ miles) long. The total ascent is 1,319m (4,327ft) achieved by 1 in 4½ gradients. This railway was steam operated until 1958, when unusually for Switzerland it

The lower entrance of a spiral tunnel, taken from the train just after it exited at a higher level on 24 May 1955.

Ausgang Sortie

Ankunft der Gotthardbahn in Göschenen

3278

This contemporary postcard shows a double-headed train drawing into Göschenen circa 1900. The Gottardbahn was taken over by the SBB in 1902. Photogloß Co, Zürich/Author's collection

Gotthardbahn.   Blatt 11.

3/5~gekuppelte Schnell~ und Personenzugslokomotive mit Schlepptender.

(Mit Vierzylinder-Verbund-Dampfmaschine.)

1. Gruppe.   Betriebsnummern 201—230.   30 Stück.

Gebaut in der Lokomotivfabrik in Winterthur, 1894—1905.

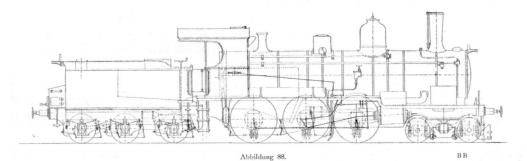

Abbildung 88.   B B

Drawing showing the Gotthardbahn Class A3/5 Dampflokomotive in detail. SBB

was dieselised. In 1982, it was converted from diesel to electric power. The Monte Generoso Railway is privately owned by the Migros organisation; this had started in 1925 when its founder, Gottlieb Duttweiler, established four mobile shops working the streets of Zürich. Today Migros is a huge organisation with 570 stores, 80 mobile shops and 270 petrol filling stations plus banking, insurance, printing and publishing, and leisure interests — the Monte Generoso Railway falling within the latter category.

The SBB runs a service to take cars through the Gotthard Tunnel. This is particularly useful in winter when the alpine passes are blocked by snow. This view shows cars loaded ready at Göschenen on 18 June 1958. Note the variety of cars; these include a Humber Super Snipe, Ford Zephyr, Messerschmitt bubble car, Mercedes Benz, Opel and a Peugeot 403. In the background there is a PTT-Verwaltung, Bahnpostwagen (clerestory post office van).

The next important place after coming through the tunnel is Bellinzona, which is 170km (106 miles) from Luzern. The SBB Works are here and the picture shows the Works entrance on 18 June 1958 — beautiful scenery and a very clean environment — very different to how British Works looked in 1958.

FFS Akkumulatortraktor (battery shunter) No Ta51 was the Bellinzona Works shunter on 18 June 1958. It was built by AEG, Berlin, and entered service in 1914; it was used during the later construction of the Simplon Tunnel.

SBB Class C5/6 2-10-0 Güterzugslokomotive mit Schlepptender No 2956. This locomotive was built by SLM in 1914 — Works No 2493 — and is seen on an Italian-bound freight at Bellinzona on 18 June 1958. At this time steam locomotives worked a number of freight trains in very dry summers when hydroelectricity was in short supply.

SBB Class Eb3/5 No 5814, built by SLM in 1911 (Works No 2215), at Giubiasco on a stopping train from Luino to Bellinzona on 8 June 1958. Note the vintage rolling stock: three six-wheel coaches and one four-wheel van at the rear.

SBB Class Be6/8^{II} No 13254, built by SLM in 1919 (Works No 2674), heads a northbound freight train at Giubiasco on 8 June 1958. These locomotives were known as 'Crocodiles'.

Schweizerische Bundesbahnen
Zugförderungs- und Werkstättedienst

Be $^6/_8$^{II} 13251-59, 61, 63-65

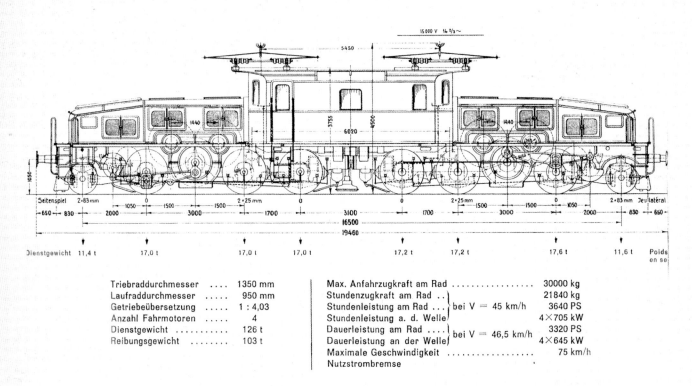

Triebraddurchmesser	1350 mm	
Laufraddurchmesser	950 mm	
Getriebeübersetzung	1 : 4,03	
Anzahl Fahrmotoren	4	
Dienstgewicht	126 t	
Reibungsgewicht	103 t	

Max. Anfahrzugkraft am Rad	30000 kg
Stundenzugkraft am Rad ..	21840 kg
Stundenleistung am Rad ... bei V = 45 km/h	3640 PS
Stundenleistung a. d. Welle	4×705 kW
Dauerleistung am Rad .... bei V = 46,5 km/h	3320 PS
Dauerleistung an der Welle	4×645 kW
Maximale Geschwindigkeit	75 km/h
Nutzstrombremse	

Drawing and technical details of SBB Class Be6/8^{II}. SBB

SBB Class Tem[1] No 70, which was later renumbered 267. The locomotive was built by SLM in 1955 and is seen at Giubiasco on 8 June 1958. As the tractor was both electric and diesel powered, it could run onto sidings where there were no overhead wires.

Schweizerische Bundesbahnen
Zugförderungs- und Werkstättedienst

Tem[1] 251-275
(früher 54—78)

15 000 V 16²⁄₃ ~

Triebraddurchmesser	950 mm
Getriebeübersetzung	1 : 7,42
Gewicht	15 t
Eingestellte Höchstleistung des Dieselmotors . .	90 PS
bei	1800 U/min
Brennstoffbehälter	100 l
Rangierbremse	
Anhängerbremse	
Handspindelbremse	

	Betrieb mit	
	Fahrleitung	Dieselmotor
Max. Anfahrzugkraft am Rad	3700 kg	3200 kg
Stundenzugkraft am Rad	1500 kg	=
Stundenleistung am Rad	120 PS	70 PS
Stundenleistung an der Welle	90 kW	54 kW
bei V ==	22 km/h	13 km/h
Maximale Geschwindigkeit	60 km/h	
» » als Anh.-fahrzeug .	65 km/h	=

Inbetriebsetzung 1950—57
Baufirmen: Tuchschmid, SBB (Yv), BBC, MFO und Saurer

Drawing and technical details of SBB Class Tem[1]. SBB

*At Locarno we see SBB
Doppelschnelltriebwagen
(high-speed twin railcar)
Class RBe4/8 No 651,
built by SWS in 1939,
in a siding, having arrived
from Bellinzona on
8 June 1958.*

*Drawing and technical details
of SBB Class RBe4/8.
SBB*

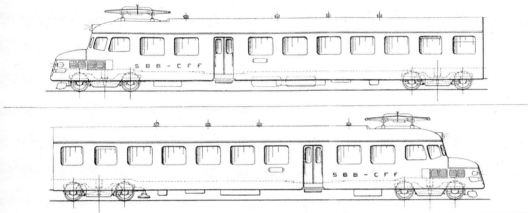

SCHWEIZERISCHE
BUNDESBAHNEN

*Schweizerische
Wagonsfabrik Schlieren
S.A. des Ateliers de Sécheron
AG. Brown, Boveri & Cie.
Maschinenfabrik Oerlikon*

RBe 4/8 651   1939

Gemischter Verkehr

TS 42

Spurweite	1435 mm	Dienstgewicht	92,6 t	Geschw'keit b.Stund'zugkraft	115 km/h	Fahrdrahtspannung	15 000 V	Radstand total	43 100 mm
Triebrad-Durchmesser	900 mm	Reibungsgewicht	45,2 t	Stundenleistung	1140 PS	Frequenz	16²/₃ Hz	BBC-Federantrieb	
Laufrad-Durchmesser	900 mm	Max.Anfahrzugkraft am Rad	4600 kg	Max. Geschwindigkeit	150 km/h	Max. Motorspannung	400 Volt	Anzahl Sitzplätze	118
Übersetzungsverhältnis	1:2,64	Stundenzugkraft	2650 kg	Anzahl Triebmotoren	4	Länge über Puffer	46 200 mm	Buffet	

*A Centovalli train at Locarno
on 25 May 1955. Motive
power is provided by Class
ABDe4/4 No 11, built by
Società Italiana Carminati
of Milan in 1923. The train
is formed of an assortment
of four-wheel trailers.*

25

During 1959, the Centovalli
Railway placed two three-car
articulated units in service,
with another two to follow.
They were built by Schindler
Waggon AG, Pratteln,
Switzerland, and the bogies
were built by Brown Boveri.
Class ABe8/8 No 22 is
pictured. Railway Gazette

Above: Ferrovie Autolinee Regionali
Ticinse (FART)/Società Subalpina
di Imprese Ferroviarie (SSIF) joint
line (Centovalli) Class Abe4/4Pp
No 84 Creveggia, which was built
by OFV/Corifer in 2007, at Ponte
Brolla (9km from Locarno).
W. R. O. Bird

A view of Locarno on 25 May
1955, showing the narrow street and
tramway with a tram in the distance.
The 4.61km long metre-gauge line
opened on 3 July 1908 and ceased
to operate on 30 April 1960.

*SBB Class Ce6/8
No 14301, built in 1925
(Works No 3072), is seen
on a personen und güterzug
(mixed train) at Lugano
on 25 May 1955.*

*Below: The tram depot
of Azienda Comunale del
Traffico Citta di Lugano
(City of Lugano Municipal
Transport Company)
is pictured on
12 June 1958.*

*The very picturesque terminus
of the tramway at Paradiso,
photographed on 12 June
1958. There was no fleet
number on the four-wheel
tram — only the destination
board showing route 1.
The driver and conductor
appear to be enjoying a siesta
between trips.*

27

Paradiso station — located 2km south-west of Lugano — on 10 June 1958. It shows the typical design of station in the Italian-speaking area of Switzerland. Moreover, it is not always hot and sunny, as can be seen!

This is included to give some idea of Lugano at night. The white dots in the top centre of the picture show the route of the Ferrovia del Monte San Salvatore funicular, on 9 June 1958. This line opened on 7 March 1890. There is another funicular of note in Lugano, the Cassarate-Suvigliana-Monte Brè, which opened on 17 February 1912. Brochure covers and plan courtesy of A. Trüb & Cie, Aarau-Lugano

From Lugano station there was a metre-gauge line that went to Tesserete, north of Lugano (LT). The line was 7.83km (4.8 miles) long; it opened on 28 July 1909 and closed on 27 May 1967. Automotrici (railcar) No 1 and trailer from the line are seen at Lugano on 7 June 1958.

Another metre-gauge line — the Ferrovia Lugano-Ponte Tresa (FLP) — was opened on 5 June 1912 and remains operational, electrified to 1,200V dc. The line is 12.3km (7.6 miles) in length and is currently operated by Ferrovia Luganesi. This view shows Ponte Tresa station on 7 June 1958 with a railcar and trailer in the distance.

The timber shed at Ponte Tresa shows automotrici No 2 with another in the background on 7 June 1958. The line had from new three railcars, three passenger trailers and six freight cars. The original passenger stock survived until the late 1970s.

29

A view on 12 June 1958 from the summit of the San Salvatore. showing the point where the Gotthard line crosses Lake Lugano.

The bridge near Melide that carries the Gotthard line over Lake Lugano, taken on 11 June 1958.

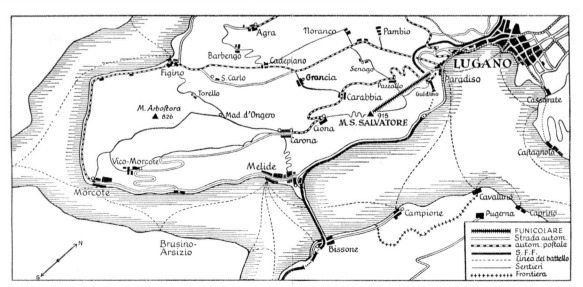

A map illustrating the various lines and funiculars to the south and west of Lugano.

We now reach Capolago, 8km (5 miles) from Melide, where SBB Class Be4/6 No 12342, built by SLM in 1923, heads a stopping train going south on 10 June 1958.

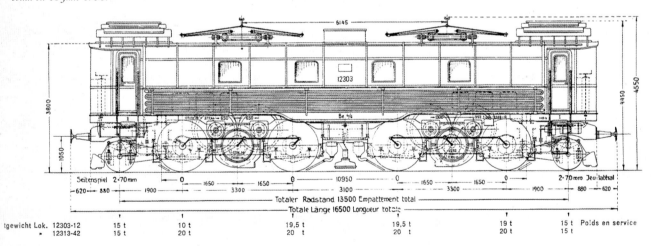

	12303—12	12313—42	**Be ⁴/₆ 12303-12342**		12303—12	12313—42
Triebraddurchmesser	1530 mm	=	Max. Anfahrzugkraft am Rad		18000 kg	=
Laufraddurchmesser	950 mm	=	Stundenzugkraft am Rad ..		9150 kg	10600 kg
Getriebeübersetzung	1 : 3,5	1 : 3,2	Stundenleistung am Rad ..	bei V = 52 km/h	1760 PS	2040 PS
Anzahl Fahrmotoren	4	=	Stundenleistung a. d. Welle		4×370 kW	4×425 kW
Dienstgewicht	107 t	110 t	Dauerleistung am Rad	bei V = 56 km/h	1600 PS	1780 PS
Reibungsgewicht	77 t	80 t	Dauerleistung an der Welle		4×330 kW	4×370 kW
Lok. 12313—42 mit elektr. Widerstandsbremse			Maximale Geschwindigkeit		75 km/h	=

Drawing and technical details of the first of the SBB Class Be4/6. SLM

SBB Class Be6/8^{III}
No 13314, built by SLM in
1927, is seen hauling a
northbound freight train at
Capolago on 10 June 1958.

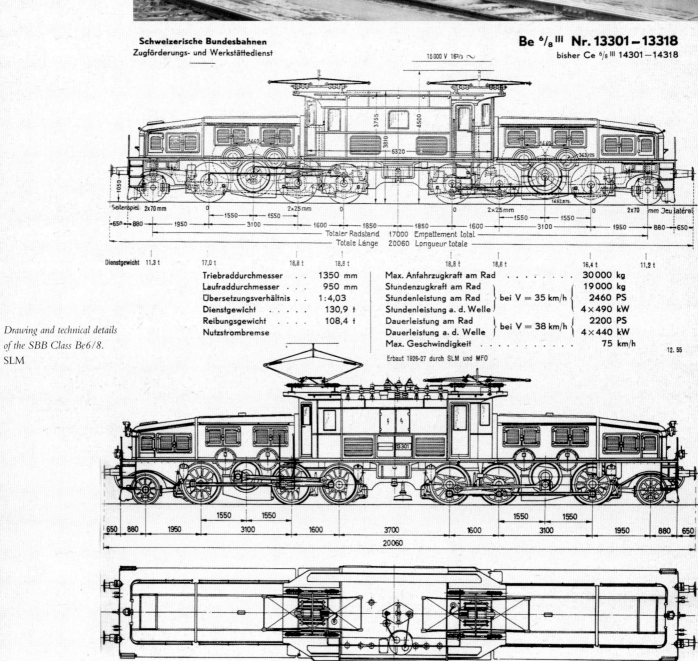

Schweizerische Bundesbahnen
Zugförderungs- und Werkstättedienst

Be ⁶/₈ ᴵᴵᴵ Nr. 13301–13318
bisher Ce ⁶/₈ ᴵᴵᴵ 14301–14318

Triebraddurchmesser . .	1350 mm
Laufraddurchmesser . . .	950 mm
Übersetzungsverhältnis . .	1:4,03
Dienstgewicht	130,9 t
Reibungsgewicht	108,4 t
Nutzstrombremse	

Max. Anfahrzugkraft am Rad	30 000 kg
Stundenzugkraft am Rad	19 000 kg
Stundenleistung am Rad } bei V = 35 km/h {	2460 PS
Stundenleistung a. d. Welle	4×490 kW
Dauerleistung am Rad } bei V = 38 km/h {	2200 PS
Dauerleistung a. d. Welle	4×440 kW
Max. Geschwindigkeit	75 km/h

Erbaut 1926-27 durch SLM und MFO

12. 55

Drawing and technical details
of the SBB Class Be6/8.
SLM

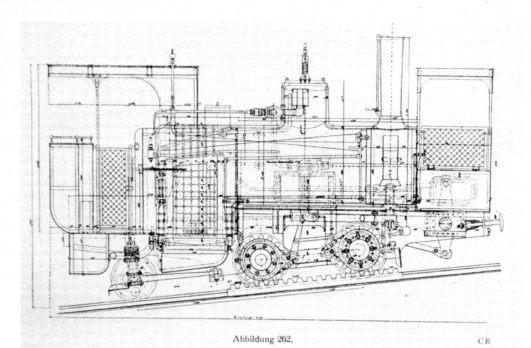

Abbildung 262.   CB

Six 0-4-2 rack tanks were built by SLM (Works Nos 589, 604-608) for the Monte Generoso Railway in 1890. Note the luggage compartment at the front.
SLM

16376 Monte Generoso — Ferrovia e Grd. Hôtel Generoso

No 6 is seen pushing a single carriage up Monte Generoso. Note again the luggage compartment in front of the smokebox.
Gebr Wehrli, Kilchberg, Zürich

Capolago station — starting point for the Monte Generoso Railway — pictured circa 1910, with rack tank No 7 about to push the single-coach train up the mountain.
MYAR

Ferrovie del Monte Generoso diesel railcar No 3 at Capolago, next to the main line, on 10 June 1958. This unit was built in 1957 by the Swiss Industrial Co (SIG). The rack line crosses over the Gotthard line by means of a bridge prior to its journey to the summit. Note the SBB semaphore signals and also the very wet weather.

THE SIMPLON LINE AND ITS ENVIRONS

159 Iselle. Entrée du tunnel du Simplon. 13 oct 1910 :

An old postcard, dated 13 October 1910, showing the Italian portal of the Simplon Tunnel. The locomotive emerging from the main tunnel appears to be one of the 'Fb3/5' class. Phototypie Co, Neuchâtel

P LANS for the construction of the Simplon Tunnel, on the Vallorbe-Lausanne-Montreux-St Maurice-Brig-Domodossola route, really started after the merger of the Jura-Simplon Railway on 1 January 1890. A contract was signed in September 1893 and on 25 November 1895 agreement was reached with the Italian Government to construct the tunnel. Work started on 1 August 1898 at Brig, and at Iselle (Italy) on 16 August 1898. The principal single tunnel was bored to full size but a parallel second tunnel of smaller bore was undertaken at the same time. This method — the idea of the contractors Brandt, Brandau of Hamburg — gave better ventilation and drainage. There was a connection between the tunnels and water for the hydraulic boring machinery, and other apparatus provided fresh air to Tunnel 1 via the smaller one. The Simplon Tunnel was opened on 1 June 1906 and 3,300V three-phase electric traction was employed. On 2 March 1930, the line voltage was changed between Brig and Iselle to the standard SBB 15,000V $16^2/_3$Hz and on 15 May 1930 the line between Iselle and Domodossola was also converted. In December 1912, it was decided to convert the smaller tunnel to full size but the work was disrupted by World War 1 and was not completed until 4 December 1921 and opened on 16 October 1922.

Continued on page 40

Class Fb3/5 Drehstromlokomotive der BBC/SBB – Strecke durch den Simplon (three-phase loco built for the Simplon line) using twin bow collectors. SBB

The Swiss portal of the Simplon Tunnel pictured after 1921. At this time the Simplon was the longest full-size tunnel in the world at 19.71km (12¼ miles) in length. SBB

Lausanne is 46km from
Vallorbe (the frontier station)
and this picture shows the
former, which was rebuilt
between 1912 and 1916.
SBB

South-east on the Simplon
line from Lausanne along
Lake Geneva (Lake Léman)
we come to Montreux.
The station, built between
1896 and 1902, was further
extended in 1903 to
accommodate the metre-gauge
Montreux-Oberland Bernois
Railway. H. Guggenheim
& Co, Zürich

La gare

Montreux

Artist. Atelier H. Guggenheim & Co., Ed to..m, Zürich No. 9709. Dép.

SBB Class RBe4/4
No 1412, built in 1963/64
at Montreux, formed
the 08.10 local train to
Lausanne on 15 September
1967. These Bo-Bo railcars
were fitted with remote control
and could be used on up
to 12 coaches in push-
pull mode.

Below: SBB Doppelschnelltriebwagen Class Rbe4/8 Roter Pfeil (Red Arrow) Nos 661 and 662 stand at Territet, a suburb of Montreux, on 1 June 1954. The unit was built by SWS at Schlieren in 1953 and was on an excursion from Montreux via Brig, Spiez and Thun to Bern. These units were used mainly for excursion traffic. The two were subsequently renumbered as 1022 and 1023..

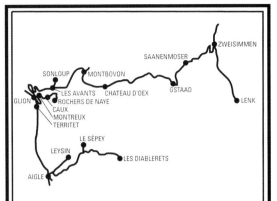

Map of lines emanating from Montreux.

The 10.39 MOB train to Zweisimmen awaits departure at Montreux on 4 June 1954, formed of Class BFZe4/4 railcar No 26 and trailer, built by SIG at Neuhausen circa 1924.

MONTREUX OBERLAND BAHN

The Montreux-Oberland Bernois Railway (MOB) metre-gauge line runs from Montreux to Zweisimmen, a distance of 88km (55 miles), where it connects with the standard-gauge Bern Lötschberg Simplon railway to Spiez (known as the Lötschbergbahn since 1997). Despite gradients as severe as 1 in 13½ (7.4%) there are no rack sections. It appears that in Switzerland where gradients are steeper than 1 in 13 rack assistance is required. The line was opened in sections: Montreux to Les Avants on 17 December 1901; Les Avants to Montbovon on 1 October 1903; Montbovon to

Château-d'Oex on 19 August 1904; Château-d'Oex to Gstaad on 20 December 1904; and Gstaad to Zweisimmen on 6 July 1905. The line was electrified from the start on 900V dc. The MOB was the first Swiss narrow-gauge line to introduce restaurant cars, and also established a record for running the only 'Pullman' in Europe on the narrow gauge; this was called the 'Golden Mountain Pullman' but was discontinued in the late 1930s. It has since been reinstated as the Golden Pass 'Panoramic Express'.

Continued on page 63

The MOB service from Montreux to Zweisimmen, pictured at Les Sciernes, 29km (18 miles) from Montreux, on 4 June 1954, comprises Class BFZe4/4 railcar No 26 and trailer, again built by SIG circa 1924. The lady with her foot dangerously near the point blades is the stationmaster.

The same train leaves Les Sciernes on 4 June 1954. A member of the author's family lived here at this time.

A reproduction of a postcard originally issued in the late 1930s shows Class DZe6/6 articulated railcar No 2001, built by SIG in 1932. Two of these railcars, the other being No 2002, were built for the short-lived 'Golden Mountain Pullman' service.
Biregg Verlag AG, CH-6003, Luzern

MOB Les Sciernes station on 4 June 1954: this was a typical wayside chalet-style building — ideal for a model.

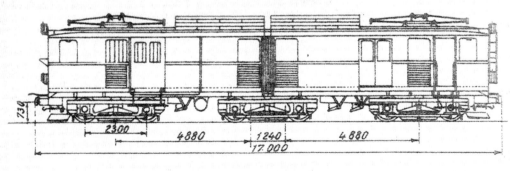

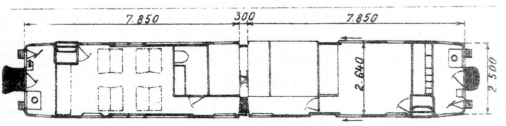

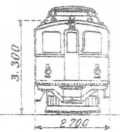

Locomotive B. B. B. du M. O. B.

Drawing of the MOB Class DZe6/6. MOB

The 11.50 MOB train from Zweisimmen to Montreux arrives at Les Sciernes on 4 June 1954, with Class BDe4/4 railcar No 3001 leading. This was built by SIG/BBC in 1944. Health & Safety would frown at this primitive crossing no doubt, but the Swiss were well aware of the dangers and always took great care. Six of these railcars were built (Nos 3001-6) and were used in pairs on heavy trains.

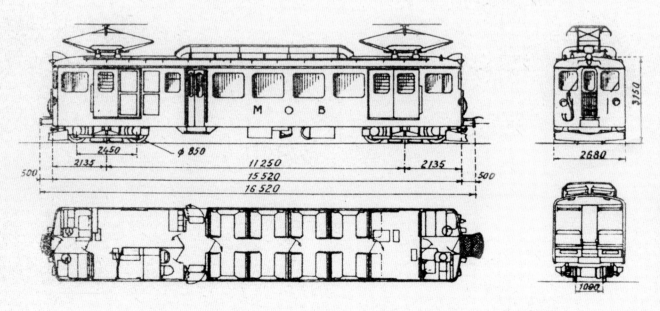

Drawing of the MOB Class BDe4/4. MOB

A double-headed service over the MOB formed by railcars from the Class BDe4/4 3001-6 series, pictured at Montreux on 15 September 1967.

The beautiful chalet-style MOB station at Rossinière, 40km (25 miles) from Montreux, on 17 September 1967.

The wonderful scenery surrounding Rossinière, with an MOB train leaving for Montreux hauled by a Class BDe4/4 railcar of the 3001-6 series on 17 September 1967.
Inset left, Second-class ticket, costing SFr 1.20, from Rossinière to Château-d'Oex dated 17 September 1967.

An MOB train arrives from Montreux hauled by one the older railcars, probably a Class BFZe4/4 still in service, on 17 September 1967.

A view from the MOB, looking back from the leading railcar, No 3001, on a double-headed train on 18 September 1967.

Opposite page left and above: Two typical MOB trains in the delightful countryside near Château-d'Oex on 18 September 1967.

The MOB station at Château-d'Oex, 46km (28.6 miles) from Montreux, on 18 September 1967.

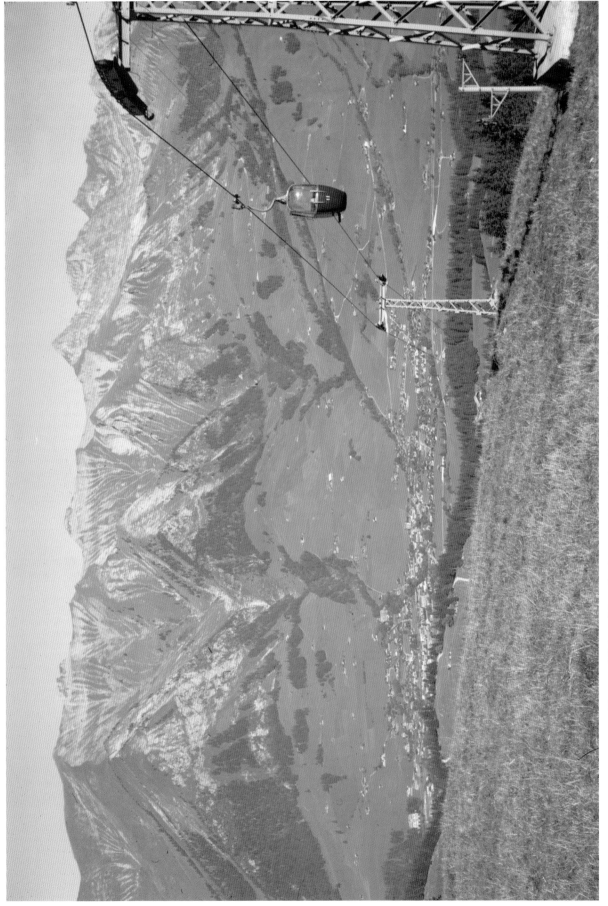

The view of Château-d'Oex taken from La Montagnette (1,700m [5,577ft] above sea level), after having travelled by cable car and the Télécabine shown in the picture, on 16 September 1967.

Another wayside MOB station, pictured on 24 September 1967. This is thought to be Les Granges, which is 3km (2 miles) from Château-d'Oex. Note the station furniture, including milk churns etc.

One of the MOB bogie parcel vans branded and used by the Swiss Post Office, Z41 No 32, at Château-d'Oex on 19 September 1967. Note the letterbox on the side similar to that carried by British TPOs.

Above: A very pleasing MOB bridge on the approaches to Gstaad, on 18 September 1967. This scene, complete with chalets, would make a very nice model.

The Swiss have always taken great care to construct engineering works that blend in with the environment.

Far left: An MOB second-class return ticket covering the journey from Château-d'Oex to Gstaad, dated 18 September 1967.

A mixed MOB train, pictured on the bridge seen in the previous photograph, approaches Gstaad on 18 September 1967. The Class BFZe4/4 railcar at the head of the train has seen better days.

An MOB Works train on the same bridge, on 18 September 1967.

We are now more up to date in our coverage of the MOB. Here a composite driving trailer, No ABt5301, is pictured at Zweisimmen on 28 June 2008. The train is working in push-pull mode with the locomotive at the other end. Note that the platform has attractive block paving.

These elegant MOB coaches, built in Pullman style in 1964 and used on the 'Golden Pass Classic' train, are shown at Zweisimmen on 28 June 2008. The concept behind this train, which commenced running on 5 May 2005, was to emulate the 'Orient Express'; it runs twice a day to and from Montreux and Zweisimmen within the ordinary services.

A close-up of the second-class bar car No Brs201 used on the MOB 'Golden Pass Classic' train, at Zweisimmen on 28 June 2008.

Another train provided by the MOB is the 'Golden Pass Panoramic' service, comprised entirely of panoramic coaches; the photograph shows one of the driving trailers. The driver is located in the cab above the passenger accommodation. The train runs between Montreux and Zweisimmen three or four times a day. The author's train had been put in the passing loop to let this superb train pass on 28 June 2008.

The MOB 'Golden Pass Classic' train, hauled by Class GDe4/4 No 6003 Saanen (built by SLM/BBC in 1983), arrives at Montreux on 28 June 2008. Saanen is a village 4km (three miles) from Gstaad.

Chemins de fer électriques Veveysans (CEV) articulated twin unit Class Be2/6 No 7002 St-Legier la Chiesaz Les Pleiades at Montreux on 28 June 2008. Although these four units, Nos 7001-7004, are owned by the CEV, they are also used on MOB Montreux local services to Fontanivent, Sonzier and Les Avants.

A close-up of No 7002 shows the coat of arms and black and white scene depicted on the centre section of the unit. Les Pleiades is an area north-east of Vevey and Montreux.

MOB Class GDe4/4 No 6001 Vevey, built by SLM/BBC in 1983, awaits departure at Montreux on 28 June 2008.

MOB Class GDe4/4
No 6001 Vevey at
Zwiesimmen on 28 June
2008. Note the BLS local
train with driving trailer
No 971 to Spiez in
the adjacent platform.

A member of the MOB
Class Ge4/4 8000 series
arrives with the 'Golden Pass
Classic' train at Zwiesimmen
on 28 June 2008. At this
time all of this class
of locomotive bore
advertising liveries.

TRANSPORTS PUBLICS FRIBOURGEOIS (TPF)

On the MOB at Montbovon, 31km from Montreux, one meets the Transports Publics Fribourgeois Railway (TPF), previously known as the Chemins de fer Fribourgeois, Gruyère-Fribourg-Morat (GFM). The line consists of both standard-gauge and narrow-gauge sections. The metre-gauge line runs from Palézieux (on the SBB standard-gauge line between Bern and Lausanne) to Montbovon via Châtel-St-Denis, Bulle and Gruyères. The line opened from Palézieux to Châtel-St-Denis on 29 April 1901, and from Châtel-St-Denis to Montbovon on 23 July 1903, a distance of 61km (40 miles) in total. The line was electrified from the start at various rising voltages, finishing up at 900V dc. There is a short branch from Bulle to Broc, serving the Nestlé factory, which opened on 29 January 1912. The standard-gauge lines run from Bulle to Romont and from Fribourg to Murten and Ins.

Continued on page 68

GFM Triebwagen Class Be4/4 No 107, supplied by SWS/Alioth in 1903, stands at Montbovon on 19 September 1967. The driver was very concerned about the mystery parcel but it was removed before being run over by another train!

Another view of No 107 and Montbovon station on 19 September 1967.

GFM Triebwagen Class Be4/4 No 102 pictured at Gruyères on 19 September 1967. This railcar is very similar to No 107 but has a different body and only one pantograph.

GFM Triebwagen Class Be4/4 No 131, built by SWS/BBC in 1943, heads a three-coach train at Montbovon on 19 September 1967.

GFM Triebwagen Class Be4/4 No 152 Châtel-St-Denis, *built by SIG/SAAS in 1977, awaits departure at Montbovon on 28 June 2008. The garish livery is in great contrast to the very sober style of 1967. One of the old MOB railcars can be seen in the shed.*

A close-up of Class Be4/4 No 152, showing the hinged destination board and other details.

The preserved horse-drawn postbus at Gruyères on 19 September 1967. It ran between Charmey and Jaun.

Gruyères is worth a visit just to see the medieval town let alone the cheese. A pity about the cars on 19 September 1967.
Far right: A second-class return ticket from Château-d'Oex to Gruyères, dated 19 September 1967.

19 SEP 67
Billet à ½ taxe
Valable 10 jours

Château-d'Œx
Gruyères
et retour
via Montbovon

2. Cl.   Fr. 3.50
A   R
01090

VEVEY-MONTREUX-CHILLON-VILLENEUVE (VMCV)

A 13km (8-mile) tramway ran between Vevey and Villeneuve, known as the Vevey-Montreux-Chillon-Villeneuve (VMCV) line. Electric from the start, it opened from Vevey to Territet on 6 June 1888, from Territet to Chillon on 16 September 1888, and from Chillon to Villeneuve on 14 December 1903. It closed on 19 January 1958.

Taken on 5 June 1954, this shows tram No 7, built by SIS in 1913, at Territet on the Vevey-Montreux-Chillon-Villeneuve tramway.

Tram Nos 18 and 2 are pictured on the same day, with a very frustrated coach driver sandwiched in between.

Another method of travel in this area is by the ships traversing Lake Léman (Lake Geneva). La Compagnie Générale de Navigation sur le Lac Léman, known as the CGN, was formed in 1873 and was the result of an amalgamation of various companies that had operated prior to this date. Here Lausanne is pictured leaving Territet on 1 June 1954. The ship is still paddle driven; it was originally coal-fired but, judging by the lack of smoke from the funnel, is now either diesel or diesel-electric.

MONTREUX-GLION (MG)

The Drahtseilbahn Territet-Glion funicular was opened on 19 August 1883, using the water ballast system and, as far as I know, is still worked by this method. The metre-gauge line is 632m (2,074ft) long and uses a form of Riggenbach rack. The ruling gradient is 1 in 2.

The passing loop on the Territet-Glion water-balanced funicular, on 31 May 1954. The line is 632m (2,074ft) in length and each passenger car could accommodate 50 people. On page 72 one of the cars is shown descending in 1967. There are supports for overhead lines and the author is uncertain whether this is for traction or lighting.

A postcard dated 10 July 1913 portrays the Territet-Glion funicular immediately prior to World War 1. Phototypie Co, Neuchâtel

*Drawing illustrating
the arrangements adopted
for the passenger cars used
on the Territet-Glion line.
This and the other drawings
of the line are reproduced from
a German book written by
H. R. Sauerländer and
published by Drück and
Verlag Aarau in 1888.*

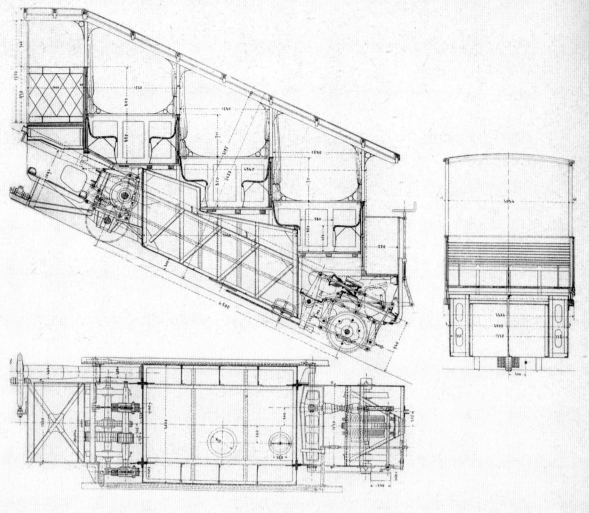

*Location map, gradient profile
and loading gauge of the
Territet-Glion line.*

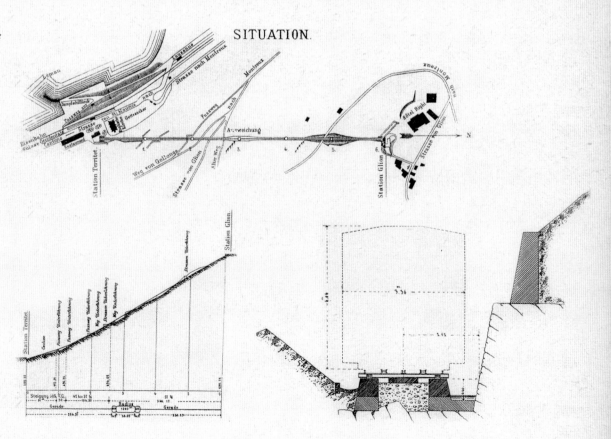

SITUATION.

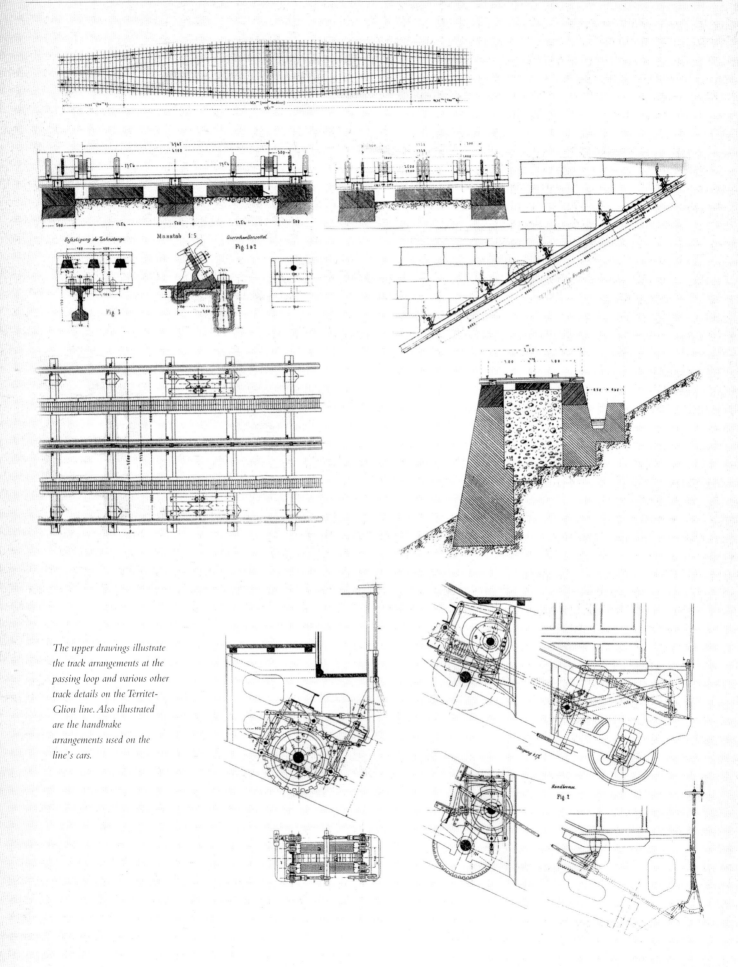

The upper drawings illustrate the track arrangements at the passing loop and various other track details on the Territet-Glion line. Also illustrated are the handbrake arrangements used on the line's cars.

A car of the Territet-Glion funicular descends the line on 21 September 1967.

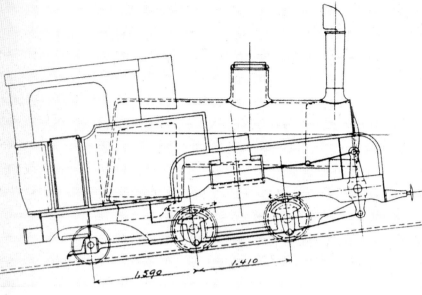

Drawing of the rack locomotives supplied to the MTGN by SLM.

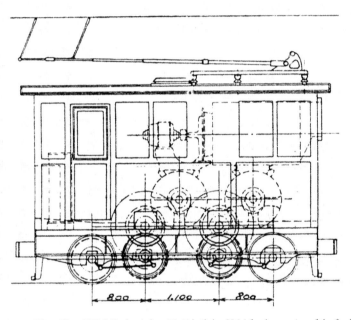

Montreux-Glion Class HGe2/2 electric loco No 7 built by SLM for the opening of the final section of the line in 1909.

GLION-ROCHERS de NAYE (MGN)

At Montreux is the Montreux-Rochers de Naye 800mm-gauge Abt rack line. This opened in sections: from Glion to Caux on 2 July 1892; Caux to Naye Fontaines on 28 July 1892; and, from Naye Fontaines to Rochers de Naye on 16 November 1892. It was originally steam worked, but was electrified at 850V dc from 22 July 1938 when it became part of the MOB. The length of the line, including the later Montreux-Glion railway, amounted to 10.32km (6.41 miles) with a total climb of 1,574m (5,164ft) achieved by means of a 1 in 4½ (22%) maximum grade.

The MGN purchased two steam rack locomotives plus four more in 1892 ready for the opening of the new railway. One more was supplied in 1903, and another in 1908, making eight in total. These were all built by SLM at Winterthur and carried Nos 1-8 and Works Nos 693 and 694/1891, 721-724/1892, 1515/1903 and 1909/1908. The locomotives all carried names: No 1 *Montreux*, No 2 *Lausanne*, No 3 *Vevey*, No 4 *Jaman*, No 5 *Glion*, No 6 *Naye*, No 7 *Caux* and No 8 *Territet*.

In order to make direct connection with the steam-worked Glion-Rochers-de-Naye rack railway, which started from the upper end of the Territet-Glion funicular, the Montreux-Glion line was opened on 8 April 1909 as a 800mm-gauge line incorporating Abt rack. This section was powered by electricity from the start.

Reproduction of a postcard originally produced in 1894, promoting the Glion-Rochers de Naye line.
Biregg Verlag AG, Luzern

MONTREUX-TERRITET-GLION-NAYE (MTGN)

The Montreux-Rochers de Naye railway, after various amalgamations in 1987 and 1992, has now become the Montreux-Territet-Glion-Naye (MTGN), and includes the funicular section. All are now part of the MOB group.

The MTGN Caux station is located 1,033m (3,389ft) above sea level between Glion and Rochers de Naye and is seen here on 5 June 1954. The only passengers were the author's parents and friend plus the man half hiding behind an overhead catenary column.

Below: An MTGN Xrote (snowplough), thought to be No 3, built in 1954 at Glion Works, pictured when virtually new on 5 June 1954.

An MTGN Class Bhe2/4 railcar, No 206, built by SLM/BBC in 1947, at Glion on 5 June 1954.

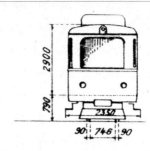

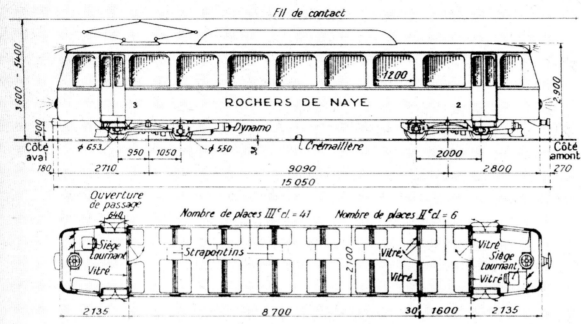

A drawing of the MTGN Class Bhe2/4 railcar, showing the class's dimension.

The MTGN's upper terminus at Rochers de Naye — 1,969m (6,460ft) above sea level — is seen in the snow on 1 June 1954. Also visible is one of the snowsheds located prior to the station entrance; the station itself forms part of the hotel.

The upper terminus at Rochers de Naye in better weather, on 21 September 1967. From this location there is a marvellous view of the Alps, including Mont Blanc.

An MTGN Class Bhe2/4 railcar, No 203, built by SLM/BBC in 1938, at the upper terminus on 21 September 1967.

MTGN railcars approach the summit on a busy day, 21 September 1967. Note the luggage wagons coupled to the front of the railcar on the ascent.

Montreux-Glion (MG)
Class HGe2/2 No 3, built
by SLM/MFO, stands at
Montreux on 20 September
1967. At the time this class
was still in use, mainly on
freight or taking supplies
to the various places on
the route plus the summit
hotel.

Above: A second-class return
ticket from Château-d'Oex
to Rochers de Naye, dated
21 September 1967.
The reverse of the ticket
states, in French, that
the ticket is not valid on
CFF services between
Montreux and Territet in
either direction.

Above: Montreux-Glion (MG)
Class HGe2/2 No 2, built
by SLM/MFO, fitted with
a small snowplough,
at Montreux on 20 September
1967.

MTGN Class Bhe4/8
No 301 Montreux at
Montreux, after arrival with
the 11.05 from Rochers de
Naye on 21 February 2002.
John Armitstead

AIGLE-LEYSIN (AL)

Leaving Montreux on the SBB Simplon line going south-east for about 15km one comes to the town of Aigle, noted not only for its 13th century castle and fine wines but also for three local metre-gauge railways. They are the Aigle-Leysin, Aigle-Ollon-Monthey-Champéry and the Aigle-Le Sépey-Les Diablerets. In 1975, all these lines plus the Bex-Villars-Bretaye were amalgamated into the Transports Publics du Chablais (TPC), which was further consolidated by the Canton of Vaud in 1996.

The Aigle-Leysin (AL) line opened in stages: from Aigle CFF to Aigle-Dépôt on 5 May 1900; from Aigle-Dépôt to Leysin

Feydey on 6 November 1900; and from Leysin Feydey to Leysin Grand Hôtel on 12 September 1916. It is a rack and adhesion railway based on the Abt system, 6.5km (4 miles) long and rises to 1,450m (4,757ft) at the summit. The steepest gradient is 1 in 4½ (22%). When the line opened it operated at 600V dc — later it became 650V dc — and then, in 1946, it changed to 1,300V dc. Finally it became 1,500V dc. Because of the Depression in the 1930s the line closed to the Grand Hôtel on 1 January 1937, but after World War 2 fortunes improved and the line reopened.

Above: A timber four-wheel coach of the Aigle-Leysin line, No 21, stands at Aigle on 26 September 1967.

Top left: Aigle-Leysin Class He2/2 No 4, built by SLM/IEG in 1909, at Aigle on 26 September 1967.

AL Class BDeh2/4 No 203, built by SLM/BBC in 1946, is also seen at Aigle on 26 September 1967.

Aigle-Ollon-Monthey-Champéry Class BDe2/4 No 106, built circa 1907, awaits departure with three trailers at Aigle on 26 September 1967. The purple/red and grey livery is very pleasing.

AIGLE-OLLON-MONTHEY-CHAMPÉRY (AOMC)

The Aigle-Ollon-Monthey-Champéry (AOMC) line is also a rack and adhesion railway based on the Strub system; it is 23km (16 miles) long and rises to 1,046m (3,432ft). The last part of the line to Champéry is rack assisted. The line opened from Aigle to Monthey on 2 April 1907, and from Monthey to Champéry on 1 February 1908. The line operates at 850V dc.

VILLENEUVE AND ST MAURICE

On the SBB, 4km (2.5 miles) south from Montreux on the Simplon line, is Villeneuve station, which opened in 1910 for passengers and apparently a separate platform was provided for the military. At St Maurice, 23km from Villeneuve on the SBB, a line runs to St Gingolph on the south side of Lake Léman (Lake Geneva) and through to the border with France.

Villeneuve station on 6 June 1954. At the front, under the apex of the roof, there was at the time a very attractive blue vitreous enamel sign stating 'Chemin de Fer'.

The 11.00 local train from St Maurice at Bouveret, 4km from St Gingolph, on 3 June 1954. The train was hauled by Class Eb3/5 No 5821, built by SLM at Winterthur in 1913 (Works No 2393). The loco had just run round the train and was waiting time before propelling forward to St Gingolph as there were no run-round facilities there. The locomotive was shedded at Renens, near Lausanne. The line was electrified a few months later and it is possible to see some of the overhead line supports already in situ.

Schweizerische Bundesbahnen.

3/5-gekuppelte Tenderlokomotive für gemischten Dienst.

(Mit Zwillings-Heissdampfmaschine.)

Prairie-Typ.   34 Stück.

Gebaut in der Lokomotivfabrik in Winterthur, 1911—1916.

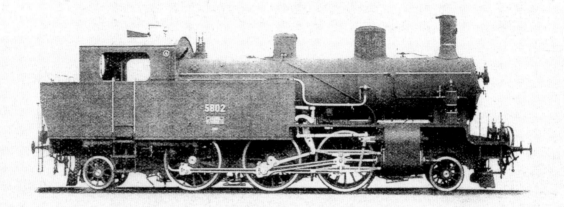

Abbildung 169.   (Siehe auch Abbildung 4, Seite 24.)   VA

Serie	Betriebsnummern	Fabriknummern	Baujahr
Eb 3/5	5801—5804	2162—2165	1911
	5805—5808	2181—2184	1911
	5809—5820	2210—2221	1912
	5821—5823	2393—2395	1913
	5824 und 5825	2396 und 2397	1914
	5826 und 5827	2501 und 2502	1915
	5828—5834	2550—2556	1916

Keine zweiten Kessel.

Ende 1922 waren noch sämtliche Nummern im Betriebe der S-B-B.

Technical information about the Class Eb3/5 2-6-2Ts. SBB

BERN AND BLS

There are numerous elegant bridges over the River Aare in Bern, two examples of which are illustrated here.

The very graceful railway bridge known as the Aareviadukt, on 14 June 1956. Construction of the bridge commenced in 1937 and carried on until 1941 when work was temporarily halted; the work was actually completed in 1942. It is constructed of reinforced concrete and is 1,152m (3,780ft) in length.

Below: Kornhausbrücke over the River Aare on 14 June 1956. The Städtische Verkehrsbetriebe Bern (SVB) tram system used this bridge. The first section of the metre-gauge tramway system opened on 1 October 1890 for a trial period using compressed air; in 1894, steam power was adopted, with electric traction from 1 July 1901.

A four-wheel tram of the SVB, No 26, operates over route No 1 on 14 June 1956. Note that the road is completely formed of granite setts.

Above: Another metre-gauge line in the Bern area in 1956 was the Vereinigte Bern-Worb-Bahnen (VBW). Worb is about 10km (6 miles) south-east of Bern, and the line opened on 21 October 1898 with steam operation; it was electrified on 25 August 1913. Triebwagen Class BDe4/4 No 35, built in 1913 and rebuilt in 1930, waits near the Kornhausbrücke on 14 June 1956.

Below: The Solothurn Zollikofen Bern Bahn (SZB) was another metre-gauge line that ran into Bern; it opened as the Bern Zollikofen Bahn on 13 July 1912. Zollikofen lies about 7km (4 miles) north of Bern, with Solothurn 35km (20 miles) further on. Triebwagen Class BDe4/4 No 21, built in 1955, and trailer are seen here running on reserved track in Bern on 14 June 1956.

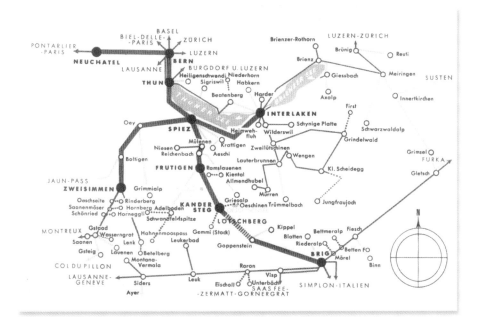

BERNER ALPENBAHN BERN LÖTSCHBERG SIMPLON (BLS)

THE idea for a line from Bern to Italy goes back to 1857, but a concession for a line from Spiez through the Lötschberg to Visp was granted only in 1891. In 1899, the Canton of Bern took over the concession together with capital from France, and the Berner Alpenbahn Bern Lötschberg Simplon (BLS) railway was formed on 27 July 1906, shortly after the opening of the first Simplon Tunnel. Meanwhile the Spiez-Frutigen section had been opened, for local traffic, on 25 July 1901 and became part of the BLS on 1 January 1907. The original Lötschberg Tunnel (14.6km), including the line from Frutigen to Brig, was opened on 15 July 1913. On 1 January 1913 the BLS had absorbed the Thunersee Railway (Thun-Interlaken-Bönigen) plus the steamer services on the Brienz and Thun

lakes. Other lines were taken over in the Bern area. This very important major line, second only to the SBB, supports joint through working with that company. Originally part of the line was only single track, but more recently a considerable part of the line has been doubled. On 15 June 2007, a new base tunnel was opened; it is 34.6km (21.6 miles) long and avoids the previous steep gradients and will therefore speed up journey times. The former subsidiary companies have been amalgamated and the company is now known as the BLS Lötschbergbahn.

Below: Spiez is 46km (30 miles) from Bern and this view, taken on 31 May 1955 from the station, shows Lake Thun which is 21km (13 miles) long and 3.2 km (2 miles) wide at its greatest extent. Spiez lies at the junction of the Simme and Kander valleys, and is thus the key to the routes to Montreux, the Gemmi Pass and the Lötschberg. Spiez station is a very important centre and there are very frequent trains to many destinations — a spotters' paradise.

SBB Class Ae4/7 No 10958, supplied by SLM in 1931, brings a train into Spiez on 22 September 1967, whilst BLS Class Ce4/6 No 308, which dated to 1921, waits to depart. No 308 was originally built as a 1-B-B-1 with driving axles driven by coupling rods actuated by crankshafts; it was rebuilt in 1954 to B-B configuration when it was reclassified Ce4/4.

SPIEZ THUNERSEE SCHWEIZ
LÖTSCHBERG-SIMPLONROUTE
SAISON APRIL-OKTOBER

A facsimile of an early postcard promoting Spiez. Biregg Verlag AG, CH-6003, Luzern

Right: This is a view of Spiez station on 22 September 1967, showing typical block bells; these were found on many large stations and were used to warn station staff of the arrival of trains in advance, before the advent of TV screens and/or dot matrix indicators. In the UK, signalmen used to ring the appropriate platform to let staff know that a train was approaching.

BLS Class Ce4/6 No 303, built by SLM in 1920, was still operating as a 1-B-B-1 when seen at Spiez on 22 September 1967.

On board a BLS Zweisimmen-Spiez stopping train on 22 September 1967. The train was hauled by Ce4/6 No 306, which was delivered in 1921.

BLS Class RBDe4/4 No 565 734-1 Ins/Anet, built circa 1984, pictured in the new livery at Spiez on 28 June 2008.

SBB Class Re4/4^{II} No 11184 (pilot), built by SLM 1969-1975, and Class Re6/6 No 11646 Bussigny, built by SLM 1975-1980, on a freight train as it passes through Spiez on 28 June 2008. No 11646 will be renumbered 620 046-3 under the new UIC (Union Internationale des Chemins de Fer) numbering system.

BLS No 420 504-3
(formerly SBB Class Re4/4^{II}
No 11123) at the head of
a train at Spiez on 30 June
2008. The first coach behind
No 504 is reminiscent of
the British Rail blue period.

At the other end of the train
headed by No 504-3 in
the previous photograph
was driving trailer No 913.

BLS No 465 001-6 Simplon/Sempione, built by SLM in 1994, in a special livery celebrating SLM's 125th anniversary. SLM

Cisalpino AG was jointly formed by the Italian FS and by SBB in November 1993. Services ran from Zürich, Luzern, Bern and Basel to destinations in Italy and the Balkans. The stock provided for the service was built in Italy by Fiat Ferroviaria Savigliano and is of the 'Pendolino' type. They worked on both the Italian dc and the Swiss ac voltage. Set ETR No 470-053 is shown here at Spiez on 30 June 2008. However, problems with the type and long delays in the acquisition of the successor Class 610 led to the termination of the agreement in late 2009. Although Cisalpino AG still exists as a company and still owns the rolling stock, FS and SBB now lease the stock required from the company for their services.

BLS Class Re4/4 (Re425) No 191 Reichenbach, *built by SLM in 1982, heads a Spiez-Zweisimmen service at Spiez on 30 June 2008 in pristine condition. Note the SBB double-deck coaches alongside.*

BLS Class Re4/4 (Re425) No 163 Grenchen, *built by SLM in 1967, is stabled at Spiez on 30 June 2008.*

BLS No 420 511-8 (ex-SBB Re4/4^{II} No 11105), built by SLM in 1964 as one of the prototypes of the class, in green livery on a stopping train at Spiez on 1 July 2008.

BLS driving trailer No 988 is on a push-pull service to Zweisimmen at Spiez on 1 July 2008. In the background, running light engine, is BLS Class Re4/4 (Re425) No 164 Lengnau, which was built by SLM in 1967.

Below: SBB Class Re460 No 460 014-4 Val-du-Trient arrives at Spiez in the evening sunshine on 28 June 2008. These express locomotives were introduced for the 'Bahn 2000' project in 1991. They can work in push-pull mode with up to 10 coaches.

BLS Cargo is 45% owned by Deutsche Bahn and works routes from Italy to Mannheim. Class Re485 No 185 536-0, seen at Spiez on 1 July 2008, hauling the vehicles shown on page 94 top left, was on hire from Angel Trains Cargo. It is in the new BLS livery and also has the new UIC number on the side (ie 94 80 0 185 536-0). This new system is described in the appendices (see page 203).

Above: No 185 536 was hauling Nos Te12 (new 1950), Tm71 (1975), Tm72 (1974), Te14 (1950), Te17 (1954) and Te215 033-2 (ex-Te33 [1960]) when seen at Spiez on 1 July 2008. It is believed that they were going for scrap or sale.

Above: BLS-owned Bubenberg, a motor vessel operating on the Thunersee, arrives at Spiez on 19 June 2008. This ship commenced operating on the lake in the summer of 1962.

Right: Brig, 101km (62.8 miles) from Spiez, is a joint BLS/SBB station on the Simplon line. SBB Class Re460 No 460 026-8 is pictured at Brig on 28 June 2008, advertising the opening of the New Lötschberg base tunnel in June 2007. The name Fricktal was allocated to this locomotive, but it did not carry it whilst in advertising livery.

SBB Class Re4/4[II] No 11136, one of the first production series of the type, stands at the head of a stabled train at Brig on 28 June 2008.

INTERLAKEN AND
ITS ENVIRONS

INTERLAKEN lies between the Thunersee and the Brienzersee — hence its name. It is one of the oldest and most popular resorts in Switzerland and a great centre for excursions, particularly by train and ship. There are two stations: Interlaken Hauptbahnhof (on a branch line 23km from Spiez) situated on the linking canal opposite Unterseen, and Interlaken Ost (3km from Hauptbahnhof) on the south side of the canal near the Brienzersee. The standard-gauge lines of the SBB and the BLS serve both stations, but the metre-gauge Berner Oberland Bahn (BOB) and the metre-gauge Zentralbahn (ZB) (Brünig Line) run only from Interlaken Ost.

BLS Class Ae6/8 No 208, built by SLM in 1942 (Works No 3797), stands at Interlaken Ost on 2 June 1955. The first of this class of eight, when built in 1926 it introduced rheostatic braking to the BLS. In 1939, the early members of the class were rebuilt to enable them to reach 90km/h.

Interlaken Hauptbahnhof was built and extended between 1917 and 1920; Interlaken Ost was built in 1916/17.

The exterior of Interlaken Ost on 2 June 1955, a very wet day. The single-deck bus in the station yard is from Hotel Victoria Jungfrau.

BLS Class Be5/7 No 162, built by SLM in 1912 (Works No 2273), arrives at Interlaken Ost on 28 May 1955, having brought in a train from Spiez. The centre driving axle is separated from the others and driven through scotch yokes by two flanking crankshafts, themselves gear-driven by two large motors. The other four axles are driven by coupling rods.

Above: SBB Class Ae4/7 No 10979, built by SLM in 1930 (Works No 3435), awaits its next duty at Interlaken Ost on 28 May 1955. There were 127 of this type constructed; these were the major workhorses of the SBB, with the first one being built in 1927 and the last in 1934.

BLS Blaupfeil (Blue Arrow) Triebwagen twin unit Class BCFe2/8 No 701 stands at Bönigen on 28 May 1955. These were originally built by SLM/SAAS in 1935, but were formed into a twin unit in 1946. The vehicles bear the initials SEZ (Spiez-Erlenbach-Zweisimmen) which is part of the BLS system. Bönigen is at the end of the line beyond Interlaken Ost and is right on the shore of the Brienzersee. The top of this photograph was missing because the view finder collapsed!

BERNER OBERLAND BAHN (BOB)

This metre-gauge line runs from Interlaken Ost to Zweilütschinen, where it divides into two branches: one to Lauterbrünnen and a second to Grindelwald. The total length is 24.7km (14.6miles) of which 5km (3 miles) are fitted with Riggenbach rack. There are two rack sections on each branch, with gradients averaging between 1 in 8½ (12%) and 1 in 11 (9%). On the adhesion sections, the maximum gradient is 1 in 40 (2.5%). The line was mostly single but, in 1999, about 3km of the route was doubled. The railway opened on 1 July 1890 and was steam operated until 17 March 1914 when it was electrified at 1,500V dc. The BOB formed an economically important link between Interlaken and the two large valley communities from which there are connections to the highest regions of the Bernese Oberland.

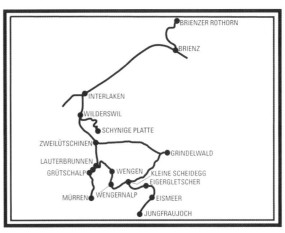

This shows the area covered in this section.

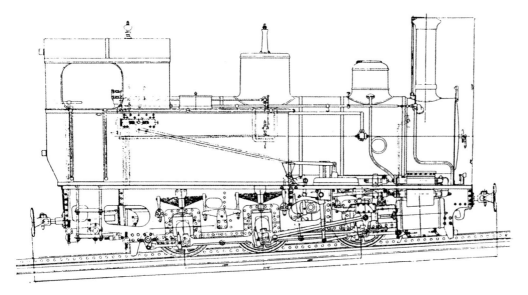

Below: A typical Swiss scene: a steam rack locomotive descends the Bernese Oberland Bahn with the Jungfrau in the centre background. Note the load of three coaches and a van in this postcard produced in the early 20th century by R. Gabler of Interlaken. Author's collection

Above: The original BOB rack/adhesion tank locomotive illustrated here was six-coupled and had four cylinders with separate driving gear for adhesion and for rack working. The inner pair of cylinders transmitted power to an intermediate shaft with pinion gearing directly in the toothed rack-wheel. A loose braking rack-wheel was placed on the leading adhesion axle. Each pair of cylinders had a separate regulator, but both were operated by one controlling screw. Both the rack and the adhesion mechanisms were controlled by an air repression brake, in addition to which both rack-wheels were also provided with separate handbrakes. The third handbrake, which acted on all the adhesion driving wheels, was used as a shunting brake. The locomotive was provided with a Klose continuous steam brake. Donald Binns collection

Left: This small rack/adhesion locomotive Eiger had been built in 1893 by SLM (Works No 797) and became No 11 in the BOB list. Donald Binns collection

The 10.30 BOB train from Interlaken Ost approaches Zweilütschinen on 29 May 1955 hauled by Class HGe3/3 No 27, built by SLM in 1914. Note the very delicate and ornate overhead support columns.

BOB Triebwagen Class ABeh4/4 No 303, built by SLM in 1949 (Works No 3972), stands at Wilderswil, 3km (1.9 miles) from Interlaken Ost, on 29 May 1955.

Wilderswil from the slopes of the Schynige Platte. The train is the 09.05 BOB service from Lauterbrünnen to Interlaken Ost, hauled by a Class HGe3/3 on 29 May 1955. During conversation with one of the drivers, he commented: 'It is rumoured that there was consultation with the GWR about the livery of the BOB.' I wonder!

BOB Triebwagen Class ABeh 4/4 No 307 Wilderswil, built by SLM/BBC in 1965, awaits departure from Interlaken Ost on 29 June 2008. Note the sparkling new livery — very different from that of 1955

SCHYNIGE PLATTE BAHN (SPB)

Some 3km south of Interlaken, in the heart of the Jungfrau region, the Schynige Platte (1,967m ([6,454ft])) provides a popular vantage point from which an all-round view of the Bernese high alps is possible. Passengers arrive from Interlaken Ost at Wilderswil on the Berner Oberland Bahn (BOB) and change trains for the Schynige Platte Bahn. This is a 800mm-gauge Riggenbach/Pauli rack line 7.2km (4½ miles) in length that climbs more than 1,371m (4,500ft) by a 1 in 4 (25%) ruling gradient. Opened on 14 June 1893, it was taken over by the BOB in 1895, with electrification at 1,500V dc taking place in 1914. Next to the summit station is the entrance to the Alpine Botanical Garden,

Below: SPB Class H2/3 No 1, built by SLM in 1891 (Works No 692), stands out of use at Wilderswil on 27 May 1955 alongside a van and snowplough.

with more than 500 varieties of plants. In the days before the Wengernalpbahn (WAB) was modified, locomotives and rolling stock were exchanged between the summer operation of the Schynige Platte Bahn and the winter sports area of the Wengernalpbahn. When the latter's old stock became surplus the best of it was transferred to the SPB and assorted liveries were evident, with a mixture of BOB brown, WAB green and SPB red and cream. One steam locomotive — Class H2/3 No 5 (SLM; 1894) — is used in winter for maintenance when the overhead lines are dismantled, and of course for rail specials in summer.

A facsimile of an SPB advertising postcard (1897). Biregg Verlag AG, CH-6003, Luzern

The 09.37 SPB train to the summit awaits departure from Wilderswil on 27 May 1955. The train will be propelled by Class He2/2 No 14, built by SLM in 1914 (Works No 2349), with passenger accommodation provided by trailer No C4/21.

An SPB train stands at the summit on 2 June 1955, formed of Class He2/2 No 12, built by SLM in 1914 (Works No 2347), with two trailers. The entrance to the Alpine Botanical Garden can be seen in the background. This station was also a post office, as were many other mountain stations in Switzerland.

The rear view of the same train (as above) at the summit on 2 June 1955, showing trailer No C4/3 to good effect. The blinds were mostly for shade and probably courting couples.

With the Jungfrau in the distance a Wengernalpbahn train is ascending. The locomotive appears to be one of the batch built by SLM in 1895. A very similar locomotive from the same manufacturer and also built in 1895 (Works No 925) is No 3 Wyddfa on the Snowdon Mountain Railway. These locos could be adapted to run on different rack systems. The card was produced by R. Gabler of Interlaken circa 1909.
Author's collection

WAB Triebwagen Class BCFhe4/4 (now Class BDhe4/4) No 105, built by SLM (Works No 4045) and BBC (Works No 4578) in 1950, awaits departure from Lauterbrünnen on 1 June 1955.

WENGERNALPBAHN (WAB)

The Wengernalpbahn leads up to the Jungfraubahn. It runs from both Lauterbrünnen and Grindelwald to the junction at Kleine Scheidegg. The section between Lauterbrünnen and Scheidegg opened on 20 June 1893 and was electrified on 3 July 1909, being originally steam operated. A second line starting from Grindelwald to Scheidegg opened for electric working on 14 June 1910, providing a quicker and more reliable ascent especially in winter. The section from Lauterbrünnen to Scheidegg is 10.48km (6.51 miles) in length, climbing 1,264m (4,147ft), whilst that from Grindelwald to Scheidegg is 8.64km (5.37 miles) in length and climbs 1,117m (3,665ft). During the period from 1948 to 1951 an extensive renovation programme was carried out; this included the purchase of seven high-speed railmotor cars and the building of a shunt back on Kleine Scheidegg, which together cost some SFr 3 million. In addition, a second snowplough was acquired and new locomotive sheds were built in Lauterbrünnen and Grindelwald. The gauge is 800mm and the line uses the Riggenbach/Pauli rack system on a gradient of 1 in 4 (25%), operating at 1,500V dc. It is considered to be the longest rack line in Europe and probably in the world. Kleine Scheidegg is 2,061m (6,762ft) above sea level.

WAB Class He2/2 No 58, supplied by SLM in 1929, arrives at Kleine Scheidegg from Lauterbrunnen on 30 May 1955.

A view of Kleine Scheidegg, showing the Wengernalpbahn in the foreground and the Jungfraubahn in the background. WAB locomotives illustrated are Class He2/2 Nos 55 and 59. The 'He2/2' class was built in batches in 1909, 1912, 1926 and 1929.

Another view of Kleine Scheidegg, on 30 May 1955. The line descending to the left goes to Grindelwald and that to the right to Lauterbrünnen.

JUNGFRAUBAHN (JB)

On 27 August 1893, the Zürich industrialist Adolf Guyer-Zeller climbed the Schilthorn near Mürren with his daughter. On the way down he stood lost in admiration before the size and majesty of the giant trio — the Eiger, the Mönch and the Jungfrau. Suddenly he caught sight of clouds of steam rising into the air in the direction of the Wengernalp — it was a train of the (then) newly opened WAB slowly climbing to Kleine Scheidegg. Guyer-Zeller remembered the earlier schemes for the construction of a Jungfrau railway and at that moment his own great plan took shape in his mind. The line was to start at Kleine Scheidegg and be linked with the already existing Wengernalpbahn. The track would be laid in the direction of the Eigergletscher, from this point it would enter the Eiger by means of a steadily climbing tunnel, loop inside the mountain, proceed beneath the Mönch and the Jungfraujoch, and spiral to a point immediately below the summit, which would be reached by a 220ft lift.

On 21 December 1894, Guyer-Zeller was granted authorisation to build the metre-gauge line and, on 27 July 1896, work was begun at Kleine Scheidegg at 2,061m (6,762ft) above sea

This is the stone monument at Interlaken to Dem Schöpfer der Jungfraubahn — The creator of the Jungfrau Railway — A. D. Guyer-Zeller 1839-1899, on 26 May 1955.

level. The railway was opened in stages: to Eigergletscher on 20 September 1898; Eigergletscher to Rotstock on 2 August 1899; Rotstock to Eigerwand on 18 June 1903; Eigerwand to Eismeer on 25 July 1905; and Eismeer to Jungfraujoch on 1 August 1912. When the railway reached Eismeer in 1905 — 3,160m (10,368ft) above sea level — the estimated cost of SFr 7½ million had been exceeded, so it was decided to site the upper terminus on the saddle between the Jungfrau (4,158m [13,642ft]) and the Mönch (4,099m [13,449ft]). The terminus station is at 3,454m (11,333ft) and is the highest in Europe. It took 16 years to construct this 9.27km (5.76-mile) long railway. Electric power was used from the start, at 7,000V three-phase at 40 cycles that was stepped down to a working voltage of 650V. Power stations to provide current were built at Lauterbrünnen and at Lütschental. The voltage now is 1,125V 50Hz three-phase ac. The line originally was rack and adhesion, but in 1951 it became rack completely using the same Strub system. The maximum gradient is 1 in 4 (25%).

The Jungfraubahn remains a masterpiece of Swiss railway construction.

Below: The Jungfrau seen from Wilderswil; the author's journey to the Jungfraujoch started from here on 30 May 1955. Out of interest there are three peaks: the Eiger (Ogre), the Mönch (Monk) and the Jungfrau (Young Maiden). The idea behind their names is the fact that the monk keeps the ogre away from the young maiden. The Eiger's peak is 3,970m (13,025ft) above sea level.

The key to numbers on the drawing:
1 — Station Jungfraujoch;
2 — Hotel Berghaus / Terrace;
3 — Lift to the 4th floor;
4 — Restaurant;
5 —Footpath to Plateau;
6 — Ice Palace;
7 — Entrance to Sphinx Tunnel;
8 — Tourist Hotel;
9 — Research Institute;
10 — Sphinx Tunnel;
11 — Sphinx Lift;
12 — Sphinx Terraces (11,723ft);
13 — Exit from Sphinx Tunnel;
14 — Husky dogs / Ski School.
Jungfraubahn

The JB original rolling stock consisted of 12 Rowan units, ie 12 locomotives with a passenger coach carried on the locomotive frame at one end and a bogie at the other. These were very similar in principle to British steam railmotors. Class He2/2 No 5, built circa 1898, is pictured at Kleine Scheidegg on 30 May 1955. This train was positioned specially for the author on the day. It was, however, still used on special occasions at the time.

JB Triebwagen Class BDhe2/4 No 201, built by SLM/BBC in 1954 (Works No 4113), and trailer stand at Kleine Scheidegg on 30 May 1955.

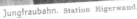
Jungfraubahn. Station Eigerwand.

Judging by the dress of the passengers, this commercial postcard produced by Verlag Wehrli AG, Kilchberg-Zürich of the JB Eigerwand station dates from before World War 1. Author's collection

On the journey towards Jungfraujoch the JB train stops for a few minutes at Eigerwand (2,865m [9,400ft]) in the Eiger Tunnel in order for passengers to see the view from an opening in the side of the mountain. This is the view through the window on 30 May 1955.

Further on during the Jungfraubahn's ascent there is another stop, in the Mönch Tunnel at Eismeer, to see the glacier through the window. This is the view, again taken on 30 May 1955.

The view at Jungfraujoch on 30 May 1955. The journey time then was 51min.

DRAHTSEILBAHN INTERLAKEN-HARDER KULM

The Valley station of this funicular railway is only 3 minutes from Interlaken Ost. This metre-gauge line opened on 15 May 1908, and the line climbs 737m (2,418ft) in its total length of 1,236m (4,056ft) with a maximum gradient of 1 in 1.6 (62%). Various figures have been published with regard to the length of the line, but 1,236m (4,056ft) has been confirmed from official sources. Trains start from both lower and upper terminals and need 16 minutes to complete their journeys. The Harder Kulm lies at 1,322m (4,337ft) and affords sweeping views down to Interlaken and the lakes of Thun and Brienz. A panorama of snow-covered peaks centres on the Eiger, Mönch and Jungfrau.

Interlaken and its environs.

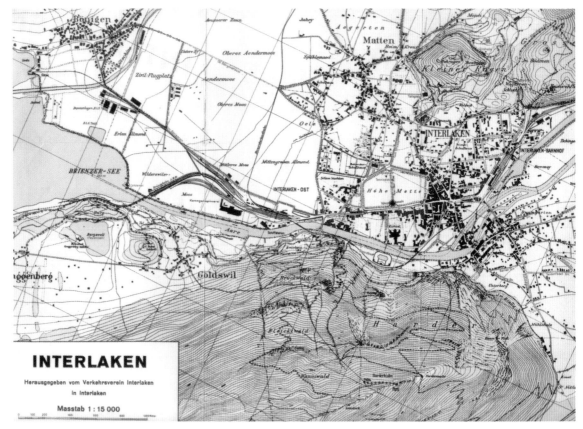

Car No 1 of the Drahtseilbahn Interlaken-Harder Kulm makes its way to the summit on 2 June 1955 with a sole passenger.

DRAHTSEILBAHN INTERLAKEN-HEIMWEHFLUH

Five minutes' walk from Interlaken Hauptbahnhof is the base station of this funicular, which opened on 21 July 1906. The length of this metre-gauge line is 185m (610ft) and the total ascent of 101m (334ft) is made at a gradient of 1 in 1.6 (62%). Journey time is 2½ minutes. Apart from the view at the summit there was, on 29 May 1955, a large O gauge model railway that had been built in 1951.

Drahtseilbahn Interlaken-Heimwehfluh No 2 begins its descent on 29 May 1955.

Below: The view from the summit 676m (2,220ft) of the Heimwehfluh shows Interlaken Hauptbahnhof and the ship canal, the latter of which was built between 1892 and 1894 to link the two lakes. Seen on the canal is MV Jungfrau, *which was owned by the BLS but built in Germany and launched on the Bodensee (Lake Constance) on 8 April 1954. The* Jungfrau *commenced service on Lake Thun on 23 May 1954 and had a capacity of 800 passengers.*

BERGBAHN LAUTERBRÜNNEN-MÜRREN (BLM)

The BLM opened on 14 August 1891 and consisted of two parts, one section of which is a 1.28km (0.8 mile) funicular railway that runs from Lauterbrünnen to Grütschalp with an average grade of 1 in 8 (12½%) and a maximum of 1 in 6 (17%). This section has a halfway passing loop and the funicular is operated by two cars. Originally operated by water counterweights, problems were encountered with freezing up so conversion to electric power was undertaken in time for the 1901/02 season. Each of the cars has a platform at its upper end to carry boxes of supplies for the village of Mürren — which is traffic-less; goods are transferred at Grütschalp by a rack-operated forklift unit to a wagon attached to the rear of a waiting railcar.

The funicular was renovated during 1948/50, with a complete renewal of the cable sections and a new driving mechanism. The old rails, together with the rack which was formerly needed for braking purposes, were replaced and a new cable was installed. However, the funicular was closed on 1 May 2006 because the line was gradually sliding out of alignment due to earth movement. The line was replaced by a cableway in December 2006. The cars for the Mürren line are now taken by road via a very convoluted route.

The second section is a 5.63km (3½-mile) long metre-gauge cliff-top adhesion railway from Grütschalp to Mürren, which runs on a ledge overlooking the Eiger, Mönch and the Jungfrau. Electrically operated from the start, using tram type vehicles, the line opened on 14 August 1891. The original vehicles were replaced by Rowan units in 1903, then again in 1913 by two-axle electric railcars, with a further example added to stock in 1925. Three new Class Be4/4 railcars, Nos 21-23, were placed in service in 1967, having been hauled up the funicular line in order to reach the railway. The maximum gradient on the railway is 1 in 20 (5%) with power being provide at 550V dc. There is an intermediate station at Winteregg.

A funicular between Mürren and Allmendhubel, which opened in 1912, later came under the same management.

A four-wheel electric locomotive (No 3) hauls a bogie carriage. The latter is interesting as it has open end platforms, an open centre section and short enclosed sections either end. This unit could have been on trial. The postcard is postmarked 21 November 1905 and was produced by Künzli-Tobler of Zürich. Author's collection

The funicular between Lauterbrünnen and Grütschalp, with the Eiger, Mönch and Jungfrau in the background. Photogloß–Wehrli AG, Zürich

*BLM Class BDe2/4
No 11, built by SIG/MFO,
en route between Grütschalp
and Mürren on 1 June
1955. This vehicle has been
preserved and reclassified
CFe2/4.*

*BLM Class BDe2/4
No 13, also supplied by
SIG/MFO, is pictured
between Mürren and
Grütschalp on 1 June 1955.*

A trestle bridge on the BLM designed to be dismantled during the winter in order to avoid being destroyed by avalanches. It is seen here on 1 June 1955.

Four-wheel STI tram No 1 hauls box van No K.71 and open wagon at Thun on 31 May 1955. The initials on the side of the car read 'STJ' but the 'J' is actually an 'I' in the old-style German script then still in use.

STEFFISBURG-THUN-INTERLAKEN STRASSENBAHN (STI)

Between Interlaken and Steffisburg, via Thun, there used to be a tramway called the Steffisburg-Thun-Interlaken (STI) line. The metre-gauge route was 26.13km (16¼ miles) in length and opened from Steffisburg to Oberhofen on 10 October 1913, to Beatenbucht on 24 December 1913, and to Interlaken on 20 June 1914. The line finally closed completely on 31 May 1958, the trams being replaced by trolleybuses and buses.

BRÜNIGBAHN, ZENTRALBAHN AND BRIENZ ROTHORN BAHN

3126. Brünigbahn. Passhöhe.

A scene on the rack section, near the summit, of the Brünigbahn. The postcard is postmarked 27 June 1909.
Author's collection

THE 74km (45.3-mile) Brünig line links two popular areas of Switzerland — Luzern and Interlaken. This metre-gauge railway was originally to have been constructed to standard gauge following a concession granted in 1874 for a line from Brienz to Alpnachstad. Unfortunately finance could not be found and this was not forthcoming until a cheaper alternative was drawn up in the form of a metre-gauge mixed rack/adhesion railway, construction of which started in 1886. Built by the Jura-Bern-Luzern Bahn, the section between Brienz and Alpnachstad opened on 14 June 1888. At this stage the line was isolated with no connections at either end to the main rail system.

On 1 June 1889, the line was extended from Alpnachstad to Luzern and in the following year it was absorbed by the Jura-Simplon Railway, becoming part of the Swiss Federal Railway (SBB) in 1903. This made the line the only metre-gauge railway operated by the SBB. After a considerable delay the line between Brienz and Interlaken opened on 23 August 1916. The line was electrified between Luzern and Meiringen on 18 November 1941, and between Meiringen and Interlaken Ost on 24 December 1942, and operates at 15kV, 16.7Hz ac.

The line is divided into three parts; from Luzern to Giswil and from Meiringen to Brienz and Interlaken it is worked by adhesion, whilst the central section between Giswil and Meiringen incorporates four Riggenbach sections as the line crosses the Brünig Pass.

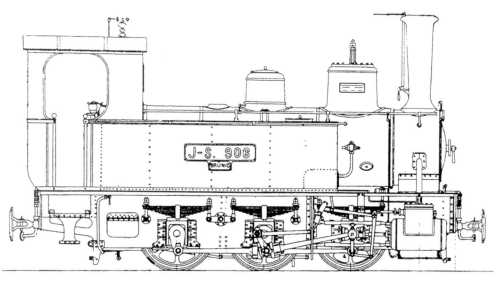

J-S. 906
BRÜNIG

Ten of these 0-6-0Ts were built by SLM at Winterthur between 1887 and 1901 for use on the adhesion sections of the Brünigbahn. The first six — SLM Works Nos 475/476 of 1887, 496-498 of 1888 and 584 of 1889 — carried JBL Nos 301-306, then JS Nos 901-906, with 907-910 (SLM 880 of 1889, 1089 of 1898 and 1341/1342 of 1901) being added. The ten became SBB Nos 101-110 in 1903.
SLM via Donald Binns

A very busy scene at Brünig station at the summit of the pass, at the end of the 19th century. Author's collection

Above: Hausenbach Brücke, near Meiringen, reproduced from Die Brünigbahn *by J. Hardmeyer, published in 1888.* Author's collection

Right: Class HG3/3 0-6-0T rack/adhesion No 1053, built by SLM in 1906 (Works No 711), at Meiringen on 8 July 1950. The late Ian G. T. Duncan

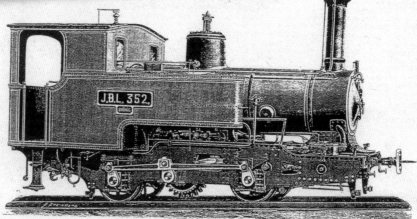

Above: Class HG2 JBL No 352, built by SLM in 1888, became JS No 952 in 1890 and SBB No 1002 in 1903. The first rack/adhesion locomotives used on the Brünigbahn, represented by this illustration of JBL No 352, were capable of hauling 40-ton loads over the 1 in 8.5 grades at 6mph. Because the adhesion sections were short between the rack sections it was thought unnecessary to provide two sets of cylinders and gear and, in consequence, the carrying wheels and the rack gear were coupled together and all worked by one pair of 13in x 18.9in cylinders. The class was fitted with three different brakes: a Rigi system (counter pressure brake) used when descending grades; a friction brake acting on the intermediate lock; and a friction brake acting on a toothed wheel mounted loose on the leading axle, this wheel engaging with the rack. Klose automatic steam braking was fitted to the train. The Engineer

Above: ZB Class HGe4/4 No 101 966-0 Brünig-Hasliberg *arrives at Interlaken Ost on 29 June 2008. Note the SBB standard-gauge double-deck coaches in the adjacent platform.*

A further view of Class HGe4/4 No 101 966-0 shows the striking livery and nameplate in more detail.

The Zentralbahn was established in 2005 and took over the Brünig line, with the Luzern-Stans-Engelberg (LSE) railway following in 2006. This latter line will be dealt with separately in this book.

In November 2012, after four years' work at Luzern, a 560m tunnel and new double-track section from the south replaced the old alignment. There is also a new station serving the exhibition centre and stadium. A further tunnel, 475m in length, has also been provided near Kriens Mattenhof.

On the journey from Interlaken Ost to Luzern, 17km (10½ miles) from Interlaken Ost, is Brienz, one of the centres of the Swiss wood-carving industry. Here one can change to travel on the Brienz Rothorn Bahn.

Continued on page 124

Soon after leaving Interlaken Ost on the ZB, the Brünig line crosses the River Aare by means of this bridge. This photograph was taken on 26 May 1955; at the time of writing, the bridge is undergoing renovation.

Below: ZB Gepäcktriebwagen Class Fhe4/6 (later Class Deh4/6) No 914, built by SLM in 1941 (Works No 3735), forms a Luzern-Interlaken Ost stopping train at Brienz on 28 May 1955. This railcar was renumbered 120 011-2 and returned to its originally livery in 2009. Based at Meiringen, it is used for testing and running historic services.

ZB Class HGe4/4 No 101 963-7 Alpnach is on a Luzern-Interlaken Ost train at Brienz on 29 June 2008.

In Switzerland it is very easy to transfer from one form of transport to another and the connections always work very well. This and the next two photographs (opposite page top right and following page) portray ships at Brienz on 29 June 2008. BLS steamship Lötschberg was originally built by Escher Wyss in 1914, but has been updated at various times.

BLS Jungfrau *was built in 1954 for the Thunersee service.*

BLS motor vessel Berner Oberland *is one of the latest ships to join the fleet.*

At Meiringen, 29km (18 miles) from Interlaken Ost, on 30 June 2008 we find former Gepäcktriebwagen 'Deh4/6' No 901, originally built by SLM in 1941; this is now Class De110 No 110 001-5. It has had its rack equipment removed but is fitted for push-pull working and, as a result, works only local services on adhesion sections.

From the train at Meiringen the author caught a glimpse of four-wheel tram No 3 on 4 June 1955. The tram operated the Meiringen-Reichenbach-Aareschlucht service; this line had opened on 24 August 1912, but was to close on 16 September 1956. The service is now operated by bus. It was at the Reichenbach Falls that Sherlock Holmes supposedly met his death whilst wrestling with Moriarty.

The standard ZB running in sign at Lungern, on 30 June 2008. This station is 38km (23½ miles) from Interlaken Ost and 36km (22 miles) from Luzern, almost halfway on the journey.

A standard-gauge SBB Spezialwagen, No 531113, containing aviation fuel on a narrow-gauge ZB transporter wagon, is seen at Hergiswil on 25 May 1954. Many of the narrow-gauge lines were able to transport standard-gauge wagons using this system.

ZB Class HGe4/4 No 101 967-8 Brienz *arrives at* Giswil, 45km (28 miles) *from Interlaken Ost, with a passenger service on 30 June 2008. The locomotive is still in its blue livery.*

The ZB's wooden locomotive/railcar shed at Giswil, seen on 30 June 2008. The private siding on the right looks as though it is now disused.

Taken when still the Brünigbahn, Gepäcktriebwagen Class Fhe4/6 (later Class Deh4/6) No 908, built by SLM in 1941 (Works No 3729), heads a stopping train from Giswil to Luzern at Hergiswil on 25 May 1954. Hergiswil is 8km (5 miles) from Luzern.

ZB Class HGe4/4 No 101 964-5 Sachseln awaits departure with a stopping train to Meiringen at Luzern Hauptbahnhof on 30 June 2008.

BRIENZ ROTHORN BAHN (BRB)

The Brienz Rothorn line is a 7.6km (4.7-mile) 800mm-gauge mountain railway using the Abt system of rack throughout. Opened on 17 June 1892, after two years of construction, the line climbs to the 2,249m (7,378ft) summit at Rothorn by a ruling gradient of 1 in 4 (25%), the total ascent being 1,681m (5,515ft). This is the greatest height difference found on any line in Switzerland. The BRB suffered financial problems, some brought about by World War 1, which resulted in closure between 1915 and 1930. It reopened in 1931 and, despite a slight setback at the beginning of World War 2, is now a successful tourist attraction. The journey takes about one hour in each direction. The line is mostly worked by steam, but diesels were introduced in 1975. However, the line took delivery in 1992 of one new steam locomotive, No 12, built by SLM, followed by two more in 1996, Nos 14 and 15.

A facsimile of a postcard originally published in 1892, advertising the opening of the Brienz Rothorn Bahn.

The cover of the Brienz Rothorn Bahn AG Report and Accounts for the year 1990. It features Class H2/3 No 4, built in 1892, with one of the panoramic coaches. BRB AG

The lower station at Brienz on 28 May 1955. The yellow sign 'Betrieb eröffnet' means 'Service open'. At this time the line ran only in the summer months and, in 1955, 28 May was the first day of operation. Class H2/3 No 7 was built by SLM in 1936 (Works No 3611).

Above: Class H2/3 No 6, built by SLM in 1933, enters one of the passing loops on the line on 28 May 1955. Snow like this would completely defeat Network Rail, but to the Swiss it was no trouble.

Up and down trains meet at one of the passing loops on 28 May 1955. At that time there were three passing loops on the line.

Left: Class H2/3 No 7 at the summit on 28 May 1955.

Below: The route to the summit on 28 May 1955.

BRB Class H2/3 No 7 at the summit on 28 May 1955, showing details of the valve gear and motion.

Class H2/3 No 4 stands on a plinth at Brienz on 21 August 1999.
John Goodman

Class H2/3 No 12 Bern, built by SLM in 1992, pictured with two panoramic coaches. BRB/SLM

LUZERN AND ITS ENVIRONS

THE Swiss Central Railway opened a line from Olten to Emmenbrücke, near Luzern, on 9 June 1856, and from Emmenbrücke to Luzern on 1 June 1859.

The Zürich-Zug-Luzern Railway, supported by the North Eastern Railway, opened its line on 1 June 1864. A link to the Gotthard line via Immensee to Arth-Goldau and Luzern was opened on 1 June 1897.

Continued on page 132

Luzern Hauptbahnhof, centre, was rebuilt between 1893 and 1897 in order to accommodate traffic from the Gotthard line and is pictured here in 1947. Railway Gazette

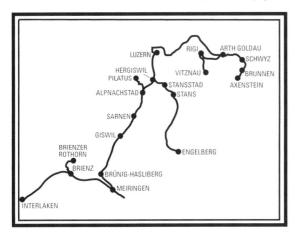

Diagrammatic plan showing the lines to be described in this section.

The superb architecture is shown in this view of Luzern Hauptbahnhof taken by the late Cecil J. Allen, a very good friend of the author. Cecil J. Allen

A detail of the central façade of the station, on 25 June 2008. The emblems on the top are in some ways similar to the quadriga on the Brandenburg Gate in Berlin.

SBB Class Re460 No 460 028-4 heads a train awaiting departure at Luzern on 25 June 2008. The coaching stock consisted of IC2000 double-deckers and Mark IV single-deckers. The locomotive was allocated the name Fricktal, but this was not in place whilst it carried advertising livery.

SBB Class RABe520 No 520 006-8 Hitzkirch forms a service to Lenzburg at Luzern on 25 June 2008. The name, in very small letters, can just be seen on the cab door. These three-section articulated units were built by Schindler Waggon (now Stadler) at Altenrhein in 2001.

SBB Class Ae6/6
No 11442, built circa 1959,
in red livery at Luzern on
30 June 2008. These
locomotives, now Class
Re610, are now in the Cargo
fleet and are used mainly
on freight services. No 11442
shows signs of damage judging
by the panel on the front end.
It was allocated the name
Stadt St Gallen but this was
not in place, although it was
very evident where the name
had been. Note BLS No 420
507-6 (ex-SBB Class
Re4/4^{II} No 11107) in
the adjacent platform; this
had been transferred to BLS
when work was divided
between the two systems.

SBB Class Re460 No 460 061-5 Wiggertal awaits departure at Luzern on 30 June 2008. It is seen in the original red livery given
to the class for 'Bahn 2000'.

BLS Class Re420 No 420 503-5 (ex-SBB No Re4/4^II No 11119) heads a train of BLS rolling stock at Luzern on 30 June 2008. This class was originally introduced in 1964; No 11119 was one of the first production series.

SBB Class Re4/4^{II} No 11205 was one of the second production series; it is seen here arriving at Luzern on 30 June 2008.

A broadside view of No 11205 illustrates the very clean lines of the design.

VERKEHRSHAUS LUZERN (SWISS TRANSPORT MUSEUM)

This museum was inaugurated in 1959 and has been enlarged over the years. The author was shown over the building during its construction in June 1958. It covers all forms of transport — rail, road, sea, air and space.

Like most museums, exhibits are changed around and added to. I have included photographs of just one or two exhibits; it really is worth a visit.

SBB Class Ae6/6 (Re610) No 610 486-3 Burgdorf *(ex-No 11486) portrayed in brand new Cargo livery at the museum on 25 June 2008.*

Above: Charles Brown was the founder of the Swiss Locomotive Works (SLM) at Winterthur and father of the founder of Brown Boveri at Baden. SLM started producing locomotives in 1873, and in 1881 the Gotthard Railway ordered two small machines — Nos 11 & 12 — for use on its line. From 1 January 1882 until the opening of the through service of the Gotthard Railway on 1 June, the two locomotives hauled the mail trains through the tunnel. No 11 was engaged in shunting duties until 1890, when it became a Works locomotive in a foundry. Subsequently preserved, No 11 is pictured in the museum on 25 June 2008.

Left: Class 2/5 No 28 Genf *was built for the Schweizerische Centralbahn by Emil Kessler of Esslingen, Germany, in 1858 (Works No 396). Withdrawn in 1899, it is shown here in the museum on 25 June 2008. This locomotive pulled the first train from Basel via Läufelfingen to Olten on 1 May 1858; it also hauled a celebratory special in 1958. Also in the picture is horse tram No 27, built in 1882 for the Städtische Strassenbahn, Zürich, and withdrawn 18 years later.*

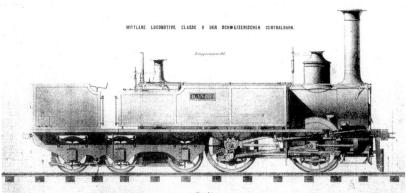

This and the photograph bottom left are included to show road transport as it is now, compared with the horse tram a century ago. Verkehrsbetriebe Luzern (VBL) trolleybus No 258, built by Siemens, is caught on service 4 outside Luzern Hauptbahnhof on 30 June 2008.

Left: VBL trolleybus No 259 pictured on service 4 outside Luzern Hauptbahnhof, again on 30 June 2008.

Above: The drawing shows Class 2/5 No 2 Basel, *which was built in 1854 (Works No 256) for the Schweizerische Centralbahn and withdrawn in 1905. These were known as support tender locomotives as they could traverse sharp curves.*

LUZERN VIERWALDSTÄTTERSEE SHIPPING

Luzern lies on the Vierwaldstättersee (Lake of the Four Forest Cantons/Lake Lucerne), and in 1835 Friedrich Knörr & Sohn founded a company in order to run steamships on the lake. The first ship was an iron paddle steamer named *Stadt Luzern*. In 1870, the various steamship companies then operating were amalgamated to become the Vereinigte Dampfschiff Gesellschaft auf dem Vierwaldstättersee (VDGV; translated as the United Steamship Company). The name changed in 1885 to Dampfschiff-Gesellschaft des Vierwaldstättersees (DGV) and in 1960 another name change came about as Schiffahrtsgesellschaft des Vierwaldstättersees (SGV).

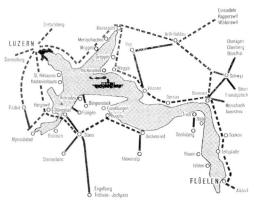

Above: As is usual in Switzerland, the majority of the ship services connect with the railway. Sea Breezes

Top right: SGV motor vessel Titlis *(118 metric tonnes), built by DGV in 1951, passes the swing bridge at Stansstad on 24 May 1954. At this time the service was run to connect with the Stansstad-Engelbergbahn. In 1964, this railway became the Luzern-Stans-Engelbergbahn with the opening of a new line linking it with the Brünig line.*

Below: SGV Gallia, *built by Escher Wyss & Co of Zürich in 1913 (Works No 583), of 327 metric tonnes with a capacity of 1,000 people, was converted to burn oil fuel in 1952/53. It is pictured at Flüelen on 13 June 1956.*

A flotilla of six SGV ships at the company's dockyard in Luzern on 28 May 1954. In the foreground is Helvetia *(178 metric tonnes), built by Escher Wyss in 1870. This ship was converted in 1882/83 from a single-deck to a 1½-decker and, in 1924/25, lengthened and her beam increased.* Gotthard *(150 metric tonnes) was built by Gebrüder Sulzer, Winterthur, in 1889, and was lengthened in 1913/14.*

STANSSTAD-ENGELBERGBAHN
(StEB)/ZENTRALBAHN (ZB)

The Stansstad-Engelbergbahn (StEB) was known by this title until 19 December 1964, when it became the Luzern-Stans-Engelbergbahn, a modernised metre-gauge line running from Stansstad, on the shores of the Vierwaldstättersee, to Engelberg, a climb of 1,851ft in a distance of 14 miles. It was a cross between a light railway and a tramway. A concession had been granted in 1890 for an electrified line from the jetty at Stansstad to Engelberg and, by 1893, an electric tramway was in operation to Stans. The Stansstad-Engelbergbahn was formed in 1897, with construction of the remainder of the route being started. The line opened throughout on 5 October 1898, operated on a three-phase ac system of 850V at 32 cycles. The overhead line was of twin wires and the motor coaches had double bow collectors. Most of this metre-gauge line was adhesion worked, but there was a Riggenbach rack section of 1,500m (4,920ft) between Obermatt and Ghärst. The gradient on the rack section was about 1 in 4 (25%) and, as most of the railcars were not equipped for rack working, a four-wheel locomotive was attached for the inclined portion of the journey. The rack locomotive was also attached to the front of all motor coaches descending the rack to provide sufficient power. Gradients on the adhesion sections were up to 1 in 20 (5%).

In 1903, the tramway service from Stansstad to Stans was withdrawn, with the Stansstad-Engelbergbahn providing an alternative service. Amongst its activities, the company advertised 'Train connection with the service of the Steamboat Co at Stansstad. Connection with the funicular railway to Gerschnialp and the cableway to Trübsee (1,828m [6,000ft] above sea level)'. The Depression of the 1930s resulted in a fall in tourist traffic and little investment was made. Indeed, after World War 2 the company had insufficient resources to modernise but suffered also as a result of its isolation from the main railway system.

In 1956, the Swiss Confederation granted a concession to build a line from Stansstad to Hergiswil on the SBB Brünig line. The company was soon placed in Administration but construction of the Lopper tunnel and Acheregg bridge went ahead and soon there existed a physical connection between the local company and the Brünig section of the SBB. At the same time, a major modernisation scheme was put in hand and, on 19 December 1964, the existing Stansstad-Engelbergbahn became the Luzern-Stans-Engelbergbahn. The original railway had been rebuilt to SBB metre-gauge standards and provided with new electrification at 15kV ac at $16^2/_3$ cycles and new rolling stock. Part of the original trackbed was realigned. Prior to this new work the line had always been physically isolated, having no connection with any other line. The SBB station at Hergiswil was rebuilt to accommodate the Engelberg trains, whilst the Luzern-Stans-Engelbergbahn provided new passenger and freight stations and a new repair depot at Stansstad. Existing train services were maintained during the period of improvement and modernisation. Five new three-coach trains, composed of a 1,080hp motor second, a centre coach (on four sets; on the fifth set the centre car is a luggage/parcels/post van) and a driving trailer composite, were constructed. Mountain railway practice continued to be applied to the 1 in 4 rack section, where the motor coaches are always used at the lower end of the grade, pushing up the rack and leading on the descent. The new trains covered the 21 miles from Luzern to Engelberg in one hour.

In 2005, this line, together with the Brünig line, became the Zentralbahn. On 12 December 2010, a new tunnel opened, which diverted traffic away from the old 1 in 4 rack section. The new line, graded at 1 in 10.5 (10%) has therefore reduced running times by 14 minutes and increased the line's capacity.

Facsimile postcard of the original StEB line, produced in 1899. Biregg Verlag AG CH–6003, Luzern

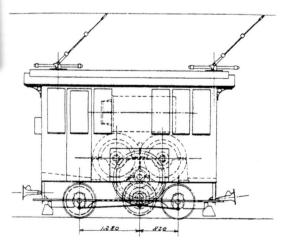

One of the electric rack locomotives used on the Stansstad-Engelbergbahn. Two motors developed 150hp each working by means of 'V' gearing and an intermediate shaft to the rack-driving wheel. A special friction switch, designed by SLM, allowed the two carrying axles to engage as driving axles on adhesion sections by means of coupling roads. Speeds were 3.4mph and 7.1mph respectively. Maximum tractive power was 6.3 tons.
Donald Binns collection

A view, taken circa 1952, showing the original terminus of the StEB line at Stansstad, with a motor vessel passing through the swing bridge. Photogloß AG, Zürich

StEB Triebwagen Class BCe2/4 No 10 at Stansstad on 24 May 1954. This vehicle had probably been in use since the line opened.

Left: A view of the StEB depot between Obermatt and Ghärst on 15 June 1956; this was where the rack locomotives were located and attached to the rear of trains for the rack section.
The locomotive in the background is Class HGe2/2 No 2, built by SLM in 1898 (Works No 1140).

StEB Triebwagen Class BCe2/4 No 9 arrives at Engelberg on 25 May 1954.

Left: Two StEB rack locomotives in a siding at the depot on 15 June 1956. The front one is Class HGe2/2 No 1, built by SLM in 1898 (Works No 1139). As the photograph was taken from a passing train, it was only possible to take details of the Works plate of the other loco, which recorded it as having been built by SLM in 1905 (Works No 1666).

Above: LSE Class BDeh No 5 (later No 140 005), which was built in 1964, heads a train at Engelberg on 28 September 2004. It is shown here is a blue advertising livery for an insurance company. Michael Farr

StEB rack locomotive Class HGe2/2 No 2 waits to set back on 16 June 1956, after working a train on the rack section.

DRAHTSEILBAHN ENGELBERG-GERSCHNIALP

The Drahtseilbahn Engelberg-Gerschnialp (DEG) is 528m (1,731ft) long and opened on 21 January 1913, with a height difference of 266m (873ft). This metre-gauge funicular climbs steeply at a gradient of 1 in 1½ (68%), with the result that the carriage compartments are stepped. The journey time in 1954 was about 4 minutes and the last part of the trip was through an 82m (270ft) tunnel prior to reaching Gerschnialp. Each car takes 70 passengers. This funicular connects with Trübsee and the Jochpass.

DEG Car No 1 descends the 528m (1,732ft) long line on 26 May 1954.

A rear view of DEG car No 2 as it descends on the same day, showing to good effect the platform used for luggage and skis.

The Luftseilbahn Engelberg-Ristis-Brunni opened in 1952; each car can accommodate 12 and the journey times is 6min. It is seen here, when only two years old, on 26 May 1954.

In addition to the glorious views at the summit of the funicular to Dietschiberg, there was the added attraction of a model railway based on the Gotthard and Lötschberg lines. The model railway was 1/10th full size with a track gauge of 144mm running on 220V ac. Nicht Gerfingerpoken! (Do not touch!) It is seen here on 28 May 1954.

LUFTSEILBAHN ENGELBERG-RISTIS (BRUNNI)

This suspension line (cable car) is 1,193m (3,915ft) long. The lower terminus is at 1,018m (3,340ft) above sea level and the upper terminus is at 1,600m (5,249ft). It appears that this form of transport, as it is cheaper to construct and maintain, will probably replace some of the funicular lines.

DRAHTSEILBAHN LUZERN (HALDE) DIETSCHIBERG

A short distance from Luzern — in 1954, a 7-minute journey by trolleybus — is Halde where a metre-gauge funicular climbed the Dietschiberg. The line opened on 10 August 1912 and was 1,257m (4,125ft) in length. It had a total ascent of 186m (610ft).

PILATUS BAHN (PB)

Travelling 12km from Luzern on the Brünig line one arrives at Alpnachstad where the traveller can join the Pilatus Bahn in order to scale the heights of Mount Pilatus.

One of the best known mountain railways in the Luzern area, this line is the steepest in the world worked by rack and pinion, and, with a gradient of 1 in 2.08 (48%), requires a special type of rack with teeth on both outer edges instead of on top. The track was of extremely solid construction, being carried on stone blocks fitted together. Opened on 4 June 1889 from Alpnachstad to Pilatuskulm, the Pilatus Bahn was first worked by steam, the 4,27km (2.66 miles) requiring 70-minute running to achieve the climb of 1,629m (5,344ft). It was electrified on 15 May 1937 on a 1,550V dc system, when

the journey time was reduced to 30 minutes up and 40 minutes down.

The success of the Rigi Railway prompted the Swiss engineers and financiers to investigate the possibility of a railway running up Mount Pilatus. None of the systems of steep railways then in use in Switzerland afforded any promise of being able to scale the sides of this gaunt limestone peak. During the mid-1880s, surveys were made and it was found to be possible with an average gradient of 1 in 2.38 and with a maximum of 1 in 2.08. A short model line was then made at this inclination and experiments were conducted using various forms of rack with vertical teeth. The application for a licence to build the Pilatus Bahn, submitted by Colonel Edouard Locher in 1885, contained plans for a mono-rail railway, contrary to the ultimate version. The upper part of a 24in x 12in box-shaped steel girder was designed as a two-part rack-rail with slanting teeth. Small guide rails were fitted to the lower edges of the 'box' to act as a centring device. The individual 10m lengths of steel were to be joined by fishplates, each length supported by two iron braces. The locomotives would have had two symmetrically slanting tubular boilers — a completely new idea — between which the two cylinders, the connecting rod and the pinions lay. Of the two pairs of helical gears with inclined teeth, the front pair was linked to the connecting rod via two spur wheels and arranged as a spun gear. Broad grappling arms gripped under the sides of the 'box', thus preventing the locomotive from derailing or mounting the teeth of the rack. It was seen that existing forms of rack construction were unsuitable for such severe grades; when the engine was working hard the pinion was liable to mount the rack and was, therefore, not safe. At this juncture, Locher suggested the use of two horizontal racks back-to-back on a central rail, and gearing with two horizontal pinions, one at each side. This system was adopted for the Pilatus Bahn, the rack rail being made in sections 3m in length and for accuracy milled out of solid steel bars. Construction of the line had to be carefully considered. It was necessary to take precautions to prevent 'creeping' of the line downhill and, at the same time, ample allowance had to be made for contraction and expansion for the differences in temperature, which on Mount Pilatus could vary between 4°F in winter and 104°F in summer. The sleepers were bolted down with sling bolts, which bound the masonry of the road bed and the iron superstructure into one solid mass.

The contract for the 800mm (2ft 7½in) gauge line was awarded to Messrs Locher & Co, Zürich, and included rolling stock and stations. Design work was carried out by Locher, Charles Brown and Messrs Weber, Hoffmann and Hass of SLM, Winterthur. Work commenced after the spring thaw in 1886, with official trials of the new steam coach in the following autumn. During 1888, a trial run was made to the summit, with the train carrying journalists and technicians. Official examination of the line, which had been built not a bit like the original plans, was made and approval given on 17 May 1889, and the railway commenced operation without any opening ceremony on 4 June. Services operated from May to October. The Kulm Hotel on Pilatus opened in 1890. The locomotives/cars were combined on the same underframe with the idea of saving weight, which would have been increased if they had been separate. Several inconveniences resulted from this arrangement, but the saving in weight was of paramount importance. The combined locomotive and carriage units were built by SLM. It was found that eight locomotives were insufficient to cope with the influx of passengers, so the steam coach that was the Swiss industry's showpiece at the World Fair in Paris was quickly purchased. This arrived at Alpnachstad on 31 December 1889.

In order to reduce the resistance as much as possible, the running wheels were flangeless, the unit being guided laterally by flanges on the central driving pinions which embraced the central channel iron forming the bed of the double rack rail; this reduced the friction, particularly on curves, and also removed any tendency to mount or jump the rails. Careful consideration was given to the braking requirements of these combined locomotive/carriage units, the engine being fitted with (1) a brake on the crankshaft, worked by hand; (2) an air-brake with cooling arrangements as on the Rigi locomotives; and (3) an automatic brake which came into action when the descending speed reached 4.26ft/sec. Mount Pilatus was frequently subjected to violent gusts of wind so, as a further safely measure, the train was fitted with clips on each side embracing the rail heads — the clips being made long to prevent jamming, the connection with the carriage frame being such that a very slight amount of vertical play was allowed in the direction of the length. According to *Engineering* for 13 May 1887, 'an engine is running daily from the lower station for conveying the materials of construction up the mountain; for this purpose the carriage part is removed and replaced by a platform'. This unit is represented in the accompanying drawings. Note the cylinder position beneath the coal bunker at the lower end of the locomotive.

Engineering for 1 November 1889 details a locomotive/ carriage for the Mount Pilatus Bahn built by SLM at Winterthur and exhibited at the Paris Exhibition of that year. This was a modified version of the original with closed cab-back and closed passenger compartments. Mechanically, the original and the modified versions were very similar, both being carried on two axles with flangeless wheels, the unit being guided entirely by the central rack. A paper read at the Zürich meeting of the Institution of Mechanical Engineers entitled 'Rack Railway Locomotives of the Swiss Mountain Railways' in July 1911 reported, 'The underframe of the coach forms at the same time a tender containing 800 litres (176 gallons) of water. The carriage is carried on two axles on three points. The boiler is of the ordinary locomotive form, but on account of the varying gradients it is placed transversely to the rails. The cylinders drive by a spur-wheel gearing on an intermediate axle, from which the power is transmitted by two pairs of conical wheels on the two vertical driving axles. At the lower end of these driving-axles the driving-wheels are placed together with their guide-rollers in order to ensure that the wheels gear properly into the rack. The leading gear-wheel is only used for the purpose of a brake and its rollers have to guide the carriage against the Dantrin rail. The leading toothed-wheels run freely when the coach is going up the inclines, and they are locked when running down hill by means of a coupling through which they transmit reverse motion to two symmetrical worm-wheels, their axle carrying the brake-disc. By reason of the high gear-ratio, relatively small braking-power is sufficient to bring the train to a standstill. The brake is automatically put on when the speed-limit is exceeded. The following brakes are arranged: An air-compression brake when running down the banks, a frictional brake on the crankshaft, as well as friction and self-acting brakes on the leading pair of geared wheels as already described. The normal speed of the train is 4.72ft per second (2.7 miles per hour), the weight of the combined engine and carriage is 12 tons, and the engine develops 100 h. p. Very excellent results have been obtained in the use of superheated steam.'

The original locomotive had its cylinders beneath the cab rear plate, but on the modified version described above (and illustrated on page 141) they were located on the underframe beneath the front end of the carriage section.

According to *Engineering* for 1 November 1889, 'All the materials employed for the construction of the trains are of superior quality; the driving pinions are of crucible cast steel; the wormwheels are of Delta metal; they were carefully tested at the Ecole Polytechnique at Zürich by M. Tetmayer. The carriage is divided into four compartments, each accommodating eight passengers. The floors and seats are so arranged that they are practically level on the steepest incline. During the three years occupied in the construction of the line, which opened on 4 June last, the engines worked without any serious wear and tear. The line starts at Alpnachstad, at an elevation of 1,434ft (437m) above the sea, and in the course of about three miles it rises to 6,778ft (2,065m), the time both of ascent and descent being about 1½ hrs.'

The following dimensions are extracted from *Engineering* for 1 November 1889 and refer to the revised locomotives:

Gauge:	2ft 7½in
Cylinders:	8.66in x 11.81in
Diameter of carrying wheels:	15.75in
Wheelbase:	12ft 0in
Total Heating Surface:	226sq ft
Grate Area:	4.09sq ft
Boiler Pressure:	12 atmospheres
Water in the boiler:	1,079lb
Water in the tank:	1,763lb
Fuel:	770lb
Weight of the carriage body:	2,425lb
Weight of the engine:	6½ tons
Weight of the complete vehicle with 35 persons:	10½ tons
Tractive effort:	5½ tons
Mean speed:	65yd/min or 2.2mph
Radius of curves:	80m

During 1905 the first electrification project was suggested for the Pilatus Bahn, but this was not proceeded with due to the excessive cost. Part of the existing steam coach fleet was upgraded when two units were fitted with superheaters.

The Pilatus Bahn was electrified on 15 May 1937 at 1,550V dc using single railcars with stepped windows. Because of the railway's inclination, the platform at Aplnachstad consists of a flight of steps, and similarly the electric motor coaches are in step formation. Passengers are then seated on the level on the steep Pilatus gradients — a common feature on funiculars but not on rack railways. At Alpnachstad, descending motor coaches are transferred to the ascending track by means of an electrically worked traverser that moves the coaches sideways from one track to another. The use of a traverser section makes complicated pointwork unnecessary.

Leaving Alpnachstad, the Pilatus Bahn climbs through meadows and woods, crossing the 75ft stone arch over the Wolfort ravine and, after a short tunnel, the motor coach is on the steep slopes of the Risleten. More short tunnels bring the train to the mountain pasture of the Ämsigenalp where, halfway up the ascent, is a station and electric traverser where ascending and descending trains can pass each other. In steam days locomotives replenished their water tanks at this point, but when electrification was completed this stop was no longer necessary and in consequence the journey time was reduced: the ascent time was lowered from 70min by steam coach to 30min by electric coach whilst the descent time was lowered from 90min to 40min. From the midway halt the journey becomes more spectacular, the line passing through a number of short tunnels cut out of limestone projections, running on a shelf blasted out of the face of a sheer precipice.

Eleven steam rail carriages were built; Nos 1-10 between 1886 and 1900, with the slightly heavier No 11 following in 1909. Nos 9 and 10 are thought to still exist — these were rebuilt from the components of withdrawn vehicles. No 9 was used as a service vehicle, whilst No 10 was loaned to the Deutsche Museum in Munich.

No	Builder	Works No	Year	Notes
1	SLM	451	1886	Superheated 1910/11
2	SLM	464	1887	Superheated 1910/11
3	SLM	465	1887	
4	SLM	512	1888	
5	SLM	513	1888	
6	SLM	514	1888	Superheated 1930
7	SLM	561	1889	
8	SLM	562	1889	Superheated 1930
9	SLM	563	1889	
10	SLM	1309	1900	
11	SLM	1983	1909	Superheated from new

Continued on page 146

*Mount Pilatus from
the village of Hergiswil
on 25 May 1954.*

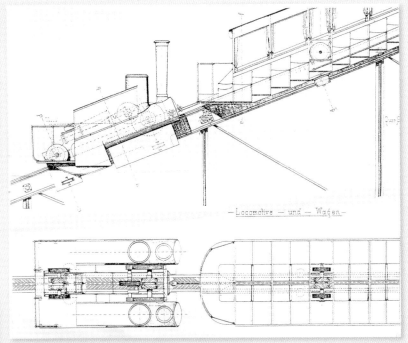

*Locomotive and carriage for mono-rail as detailed in the 1885
Pilatus Railway proposal.* Donald Binns collection

THE MOUNT PILATUS RAILWAY.

MESSRS. LOCKER AND CO., ZURICH, CONTRACTORS.

Map and gradient profile of the Pilatus Railway. Engineering, 13 May 1887

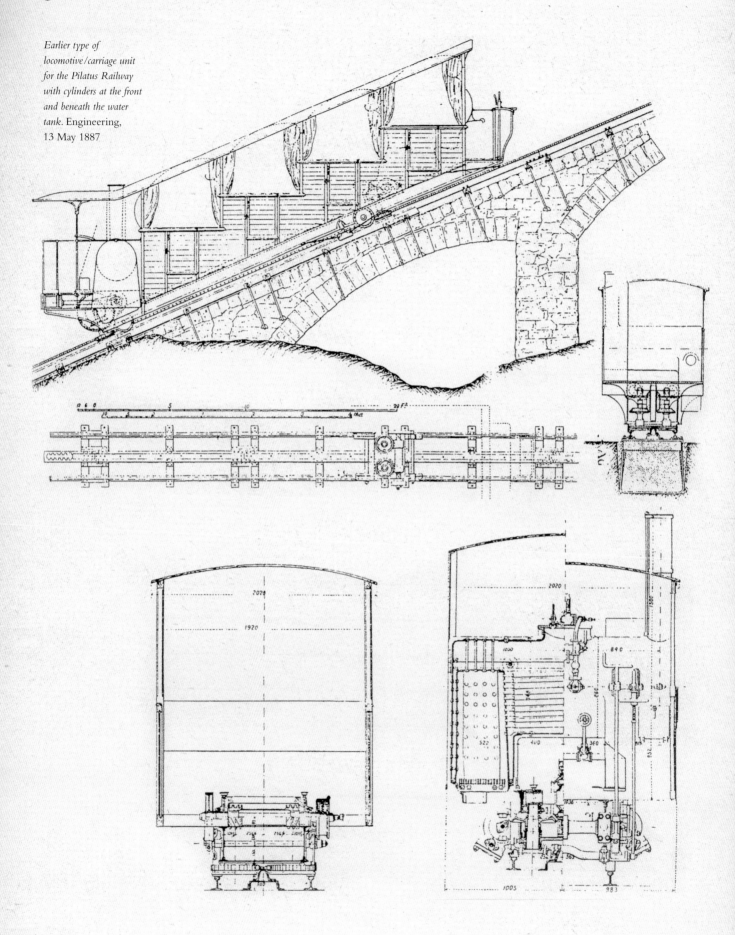

Earlier type of locomotive/carriage unit for the Pilatus Railway with cylinders at the front and beneath the water tank. Engineering, 13 May 1887

A steam carriage when new in 1888/89.
SLM, Winterthur

This combined locomotive and carriage was the Swiss industry showpiece at the 1889 Paris Exhibition. It was purchased by the Pilatus Bahn. Note the cylinder position beneath the front of the carriage; earlier locomotive/carriage units had the cylinders at the front end beneath the water tank — see the drawing on page 141.
Engineering, 1 November 1889

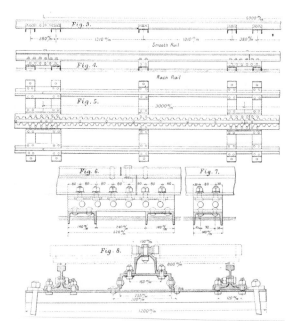

Track arrangements as adopted by the Pilatus Railway.
Engineering, 13 May 1887

The Locher system of rack and pinion drive, as used on the Pilatus Bahn. The rack has two rows of teeth cut horizontally in its outer edges every 86mm.
Pilatus Bahn

Engraving from The Mt Pilatus Railway *by J. Hardmeyer, published by Orell Füssli & Co, Zürich, circa 1888.* Author's collection

PB Class Bhe1/2 No 21, built by SLM/MFO in 1937, stands in the platform at Alpnachstad on 25 May 1954. Note the stepped platform built this way due to the very steep incline.

On the Ämsigenalp 1,350m (4,430ft) above sea level and in the middle of the 4.58km (2.85 mile) long Pilatus line there is a crossing with a traverser. The rail sections were moved into position by means of hand cranks. The photograph, taken from the cab of another railcar, shows the traverser on 25 May 1954.

A line-up on the Pilatus Bahn, showing steam railcar No 9 (1889), Class Bhe 1/2 No 23 (1937) and one dual-purpose vehicle, Class Xhm 1/2 No 32 (1981).
Pilatus Bahn

The vista from Mount Pilatus, showing the surrounding peaks and the Vierwaldstättersee.
Pilatus Bahn

This undated postcard shows part of the Drahtseilbahn Kriens-Sonnenberg and gives some impression of its gradient. Gebr Wehrli, Kilchberg–Zürich

DRAHTSEILBAHN KRIENS-SONNENBERG (SbB)

At Kriens, south-west of Luzern, the Drahtseilbahn Kriens-Sonnenberg metre-gauge funicular is 839m (2,754ft) in length. The line is electric powered and was opened on 5 May 1902. The steepest gradient is 1 in 2.3 (43%) and the total ascent is 210m (689ft).

HAMMETSCHWAND PERSONENAUFZUG

At Kehrsiten, on the Vierwald-stättersee, there is the Kehrsiten-Bürgenstock (BstB) metre-gauge funicular, which is 944m (3,097ft) long. The line opened on 8 July 1888, and has its upper terminus at 874m (2,867ft) above sea level. At the summit of the BstB is the Hammetschwand lift, which begins its journey inside the Bürgenstock and, shortly after take-off, emerges into the open and completes the ascent of 165m (540ft) in 62 seconds. Construction of the lattice steel structure was started in 1903 and completed in 1905. The base terminus of the lift is at 962m (3,156ft) above sea level and the top is at 1,132m (3,714ft). The first car was of wooden construction but, *circa* 1936, a new car, built by Schindler, was installed. Further improvements have been made since then.

Postcard postmarked 5 May 1913, portraying the Hammetschwand lift. E. Goetz, Luzern

Originally issued in 1892, this postcard illustrates the route of the Kehrsiten-Bürgenstock funicular. Biregg Verlag AG, Luzern

This view was taken on 11 June 1956, with the lift looking just the same more than 40 years later.

BRUNNEN-MORSCHACH-AXENSTEIN BAHN (BrMB)

Brunnen lies on the eastern end of the Vierwaldstättersee at the junction with the Urnersee and is also on the Gotthard line. Here, up to 1969, one could change for the metre-gauge railway to Axenstein. The purpose of this little railway was to transport visitors from Brunnen up to the summer resorts of Morschach and Axenstein at an altitude of 610-731m (2,000-2,400ft). The line opened on 1 August 1905 with a length of 2.047km (1.27miles) and the type of rack used was Strub. With a maximum gradient of 1 in 6 (17%), the line climbed 267m (879ft) with curves of 80m (262ft). It was electrified from the start and was three-phase with two contact wires. The locomotives were connected to the coaches on Rowan's system. These units had only one driving axle powered by two 80hp polyphase motors by means of double transmitting gear. The trailing axle was provided with a brake rack-wheel, and it and the driving rack-wheel were both braked. The line closed on 29 March 1969. Apparently Queen Victoria said, 'This is the most beautiful spot I met with on my journey through Switzerland.'

BrMB Rowan unit No 2, built by SLM in 1904 (Works No 1613; one of three delivered to the line), with attached trailer No 4 at the summit station on 13 June 1956. Note the use of the trolleybus-style collectors.

ELEKTRISCHE BAHN · CHEMIN DE FER ELECTRIQUE · COG WHEEL RAILWAY

BRUNNEN
MORSCHACH
(AXENFELS)
AXENSTEIN

VIERWALDSTÄTTERSEE · LAC DES QUATRE-CANTONS · LAKE OF LUCERNE

A facsimile cover of the BrMB brochure, which gives the location and route of the line. BrMB/Amstutz & Herdeg, Zürich

BrMB Rowan unit No 4, one of four supplied by Bautzen (Nos 4/5 and 7/8), at the summit on 13 June 1956. It seems incredible that this unit was still running in 1956.

NIKLAUS RIGGENBACH AND THE RIGI RACK RAILWAYS

Niklaus Riggenbach was for 20 years, from 1853, Locomotive Superintendent of the Central Railway of Switzerland (CRS) in Olten and he had much to do with the introduction of railways to the country. Part of the CRS passed beneath the Hauenstein, between Basel and Olten. On this section was a steep climb from Sissach that extended for about 6 miles with a gradient of 1 in 47.5 to Laüfelfingen, where the main tunnel began. At the tunnel entrance the rising grade increased to 1 in 38.5 and continued to Olten station. The length of this steeper section was about 5.5 miles, of which 1.5 miles lay within the tunnel. Riggenbach found that his conventional 0-6-0 locomotive could take 120 tons up the 1 in 38.5 in the open, but could manage only 90 tons through the tunnel due to the wet and slippery rails. This state of affairs result in a reduction of 25% in the effective work done by the locomotives, so Riggenbach began to think of ways of overcoming these problems, eventually coming to the conclusion that a rack-rail would be the best solution. On 12 August 1863, after trying various models, Riggenbach patented an improved method of constructing rack-rails and locomotives having toothed gear-wheels meshing with the rack. The French patent was taken up by the locomotive building firm of André Koechlin & Cie of Mulhouse.

Following this, Riggenbach set about trying to find a suitable location on which to build a steep gradient railway employing his rack system, but it was not until 1869 that the opportunity arose. In 1868, he had journeyed to America to inspect the Mount Washington Cog Railway and, on his return to Switzerland in the following year, set about the construction of a standard-gauge rack/adhesion line from the CRS, running to quarries at Ostermundingen, near Bern. This experiment proved that Riggenbach's idea actually worked and, along with several associates, he looked around Switzerland for a suitable location at which to make a large-scale experiment using rack propulsion.

The chosen location was the Rigi, a mountain close to the Vierwaldstättersee (Lake of Luzern). Riggenbach, along with his partners Naeff and Zschokke, set about obtaining a concession from the Canton of Luzern and construction commenced in November 1869. The standard-gauge Rigi Railway commenced at Vitznau (on the Vierwaldstättersee) and proceeded up the mountain, terminating originally at Staffelhöhe, a quarter-mile short and 650ft below the summit. This section opened on 23 May 1871.

On 23 December 1872, the Federal Railway Act came into effect. This still allowed private railway construction but the Federal Government took over from the various Cantons the right to grant concessions for new construction. From this date all plans for new construction had to be submitted to Bern for approval. The reason why the Rigi Railway extended only from Vitznau to Staffelhöhe was that this was the border between the Cantons of Luzern and Schwyz and at the time there was considerable rivalry between the two. Since the Rigi was started before the Federal Railway Act came into effect, the Canton of Schwyz was in order to refuse the Rigi Railway permission to cross the border. There was, of course, an ulterior motive since the Schwyz Canton realised the tourist potential and determined to build its own railway to the summit. Accordingly a group of citizens of Arth, a town at the southern end of the neighbouring Zugersee, obtained a concession from the Canton of Schwyz authorising the construction of a new railway from the Gotthard Railway junction of Arth-Goldau, up the east side of the Rigi, to Staffelhöhe and from there to the summit. Construction commenced on the upper section from Staffelhöhe to the

Kulm (summit station) and this was handed over to the Vitznau-Rigi Railway, the Arth-Rigi Co receiving 60% of the gross receipts from the operation of this upper section that opened on 27 June 1873. The separate 6.1-mile long Arth-Rigi Railway (ARB) from Arth-Goldau opened on 4 June 1875 and had its own independent track to the summit so that today there are double tracks from Staffelhöhe to Rigi Kulm. The ARB was electrified on 20 May 1907 and has a ruling gradient of 1 in 5 (20%).

In the early years, the Rigi had been opened up by the two mountain railways and there were no fewer than 16 hotels on different parts of the ridge, offering in excess of 1,800 beds. At Kaltbad a 4-mile metre-gauge branch ran along the crest of the ridge to Scheidegg, but this is no longer in existence and, indeed, many of the hotels have also closed down.

The following description of the Rigi Railway is extracted from *Engineering* for 29 March 1872:

'The Rigi Railway starts at Vitznau, on the shore of Lake Lucerne, and extends a distance of 5,760 yards, or about 3¼ miles, to the station at Staffelhöhe, a short distance above Rigi Kaltbad, the well-known hotel and establishment for cold baths … the line rises 3,937ft, the gradient being at first 1 in 14.9, while after getting clear of the town of Vitznau it varies from 1 in 5.56 to as steep as 1 in 4, the average gradient for the whole distance being 1 in 4.45. The curves are all of radius 590½ft. … The principal works on the line are a tunnel 246ft in length and a bridge over the Schnurtobel, of three spans, and a total length of 279ft. Both the tunnel and the bridge are on a gradient of 1 in 4. … The bridge is also on a curve. It consists of three spans of 83ft 8in each and is composed of two plate girders of 3ft 11¼in deep, placed 6ft 10⁵⁄₈in apart from centre to centre, and connected every 5ft by T irons and diagonal bars. … Longitudinal timber sleepers and footways are provided. The total width of the bridge between handrails is 13ft 9in. … For a great part of the length of the line the bed for the cross-sleepers is formed by cutting away the rock itself to the depth of about a foot. The cross-sleepers are 6in deep, 8in wide, and 7ft 10½in long and they are placed at a distance apart of 23ft 5½in from centre to centre. Upon them are spiked the carrying rails of Vignoles section, and weighing 35lb per yard, and also the central rack. Besides the rails there are also fixed to the cross-sleepers the longitudinal guard timber having a section of 6in x 7in. The carrying rails are laid to 4ft 8½in gauge and the whole permanent way is prevented from slipping down the steep gradient by the cross-sleepers being made at intervals of about 250ft, to take a firm abutment against masonry piers let into the solid rock.

'The central rack into which the toothed wheels on the locomotives and carriages gear is formed of two channel irons, each 4¾in deep, by 2⁵⁄₈in thick. These two channel irons are placed 5in apart, and into them are riveted the ends of a series of pins or teeth formed of wrought iron. These bars or teeth are placed at a pitch of 3.94in and they are 1.42in deep, by 1.42in wide on the upper, and 2.16in wide on the lower sides. … At their ends, where they are riveted into the channel irons, they are rounded at their sides. … The central rack we have been describing is made in lengths of 3 metres (9ft 10in), these lengths being united by fish-plates bolted to the lower flanges of the channel irons. On the curves the teeth or bars are made to converge to the centre of an arc of 590½ft radius.

'At each of the termini and at an intermediate point at the middle of the line is placed an arrangement for shifting the trains from one line of rails to another. The employment of toothed wheels gearing into a central rack rendered ordinary switches inapplicable … the arrangement used consists of a part turntable, or rather swing bridge, turning on a pivot at one end, carrying a line of rails, which can be made to agree with either line of rails. The turntable is altogether 49ft 3in long and is supported at two intermediate points by wheels travelling on the rails. The table is shifted by gearing acting on a toothed rod connected to the table.

'The locomotives used … on the Rigi Railway [are] constructed by M. Riggenbach, at the workshops of the Central Swiss Railway at Alten [Olten]. …The engine is carried on four wheels, the boiler being of the vertical type situated midway between the two axles. The boiler is so fixed to the frame that its axis is vertical when the engine is standing on a gradient of 1 in 5.623. The wheelbase is 9ft 10in. The cylinders are 10⅝in diameter with 15¾in stroke, and they are fixed to the outside of the frames by the side of the boiler. The valve gear is of the straight link kind, and is actuated by eccentrics mounted on overhung cranks. … The connecting rods are coupled to cranks on the end of a shaft carrying two pinions each of 8.67in diameter. These pinions have each 14 teeth and they gear into spur wheels, with 43 teeth, keyed on the driving or lower axle. On this axle are placed the lower carrying wheels while there is also keyed on its centre the toothed wheel which gears into the central rack. This wheel is 2ft 1in in diameter and has 20 teeth. The second or upper axle is also provided, besides its carrying wheels, with a central spur wheel which gears into the central rack, this wheel being employed for arresting the motion of the trains by means of the brakes. For this purpose there are on the axle between the toothed wheel and the carrying wheels two pulleys, which can be clipped by hanging brake blocks which are brought into action by means of links and levers actuated by ordinary brake screws on the tender. The crank shaft also carries a brake pulley of small diameter … its circumference having a number of V grooves turned in it so as to increase the grip of the brake blocks that are applied by the aid of the handwheel (nearest to the boiler).

'… a retarding power is exerted by counter pressure in the cylinders during the time the train is descending. Thus when a descent is being made, the steam is shut off from the cylinders by a handle (on the steam line mounted on the boiler) and the pistons are allowed to pump air, this being drawn in through an opening in the box connected with the exhaust pipe and being forced into the steam pipe, whence it escapes through a cock provided. The box contains two valves, one covering an opening at the bottom communicating with the external air, while the other closes the communication with the upper part of the exhaust pipe, this portion of the pipe being bell-mounted at its lower end to afford space for the valve to work. Both these valves open by being lifted, and their spindles are connected by a lever vibrating on an intermediate fulcrum, the arrangement being such that when one valve is opened the other is necessarily

closed. When the exhaust steam is admitted to the box, the pressure opens the valve leading to the upper part of the exhaust pipe, and closes that communicating with the external air, while, when the cylinders are drawing air from the box, the exhaustion opens the valve communicating with the external air, and closes that communicating with the upper part of the exhaust pipe, thus preventing dust and ashes from being drawn into the cylinders from the smokebox. Also whilst the descent is taking place, a small stream of water from the tender is turned into each cylinder to prevent the latter from working dry, and by adjusting the opening of the escape cock, the counter pressure of air against the pistons can be regulated to any desired amount.

'To prevent any chance of derailment in the case of the spur wheels getting out of gear, there are, at each end of the engine, strong guard irons curved inwards at their lower ends. .... At its lower end the engine carries a tank and fuel bunker … at the upper end there is a receptacle for passengers' luggage, this receptacle having open trellis sides. The weight of the engine in working order is 12½ tons.

'The train consists, besides the locomotive, of a single passenger carriage having open sides. The weight of the vehicle is 4 tons and it carries 54 passengers on nine seats, six on each. The seats all face down hill. This vehicle is carried on four wheels, each of the two axles being provided besides the carrying wheels, with two brake pulleys and a toothed wheel, gearing into the central rack. The carriage … is not coupled to the engine but the headstock at the lower end abuts against a buffer on the engine.'

As noted above, the first six Vitznau-Rigi Railway (VRB) locomotives were built at the CRS's shops at Olten. These were constructed with vertical boilers as follows:

No	Name	Works No	Year
1	*Stadt Luzern*	17	1870
2	*Stadt Basel*	18	1871
3	*Stadt Bern*	19	1871
4	—	21	1872
5	—	22	1872
6	—	23	1873

These were rebuilt with horizontal boilers at Olten:

No	Rebuilt
1	1882
2	1883
3	1884
4	1886
5	1886
6	1891

Later locomotives Nos 7-10 of the VRB were built to Riggenbach's plans by SLM at Winterthur (Works Nos 1-4/1873).

The following is extracted from a paper by Mr T. Weber, Managing Director, and Mr S. Abt, Works Engineer, of SLM, Winterthur, that was read at the July 1911 Zürich meeting of the Institution of Mechanical Engineers entitled

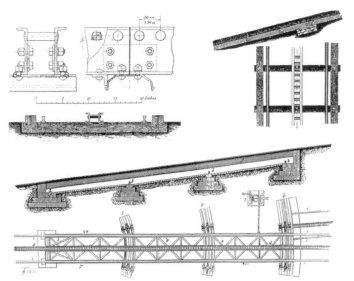

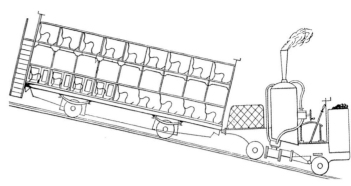

According to Engineering *for 5 May 1871, there were to be double-deck carriages seating 46 on the lower deck and 36 on the upper. Whether these ever entered service or if the design was abandoned in favour of single-deck four-wheelers is not known. The interior of the lower deck was reached by end doors, whilst the upper deck was reached by a light iron staircase at one end only. At both ends of the carriage was a screw brake comprising toothed wheels engaging with the centre rack.*

Detailed drawings of the methods of track construction and operation of the pointwork on the Rigi Railway.

'Rack Railway Locomotives of the Swiss Mountain Railways'.

'(a) Locomotives with Rack-Gear only. As already stated, in May 1871, the now well-known Vitznau-Rigi Railway was opened as the first European rack-railway for passenger traffic. The gauge is the ordinary English gauge. The line has a length of 4.38 miles and gradients from 6 per cent up to 25 per cent, the mean gradient being 20 per cent. The curves have 591ft radius. The original road was built with longitudinal and cross-sleepers but between 1885 and 1895 the road was rebuilt, the timber sleepers being replaced by iron ones, and the iron rails being replaced by steel rails.

'The first locomotive for this line was built at the works of the Central Railway in Olten; the engine had a vertical boiler similar to the engines on Mount Washington in order to reduce as much as possible the variations in water-level arising from the different gradients over which the engines worked. Following locomotives were built by SLM in Winterthur, and were the first work turned out by that firm. After eleven years use of the vertical boilers were replaced by horizontal ones.

'The appended diagram shows the vertical boiler engine carried on two axles, on the lower of which is mounted running loose the driving cog-wheel which is driven by gearing from the crankshaft. The cylinders lie on both sides outside the frames, and drive the intermediate shaft by means of connecting-rods and cranks. The upper axle carries a toothed brake-wheel with an arrangement to be used in case of an accident to the driving wheel. The ordinary brake works on the discs of the crankshaft.

'When going down hill, an air counter-pressure brake is made use of, that is, the valve-gear is reversed and the regulator is shut off. The pistons then draw air into the cylinder, which is compressed up as far as the regulator. This braking is governed by throttling the exhaust of the compressed air by means of a valve worked by the driver.

'In the latest locomotives of the Rigi Railway, which were built at the Winterthur Works between 1899 and 1902, the cylinders are placed farther toward the leading end. The driving cog-wheel, which is driven by means of gearing

A reproduction of a postcard promoting the VRB, issued originally in 1913. Biregg Verlag AG CH-6003, Luzern

from the intermediate axle, has a larger diameter and is placed close behind the front carrying-axle; the trailer carrying-axle is provided with a rack-brake. The brakes are arranged in the same manner as on the old engines, but in addition a centrifugal governor is made use of, which automatically controls the maximum speed, at which point a steam-brake is put into action. This automatic speed-regulator (a special construction of the Winterthur Works) has to be applied, by order of the Swiss Railway Department, on all rack-locomotives in service on Swiss lines. The speed of the Rigi locomotives is 6.8 feet per second (4.7 miles per hour), and the total weight of the train is between 25 to 28 tons, about 200 hp being developed by the engine.'

The Vitznau-Rigi Bahn of today is a totally modern business, with the introduction of electrification on 3 October 1937. It is now operated on a 1,500V dc supply and has an operational length of 6.85km (4.26 miles). A double line operates from Freibergen to Rigi Kaltbad for a length of 1.89km (1.17 miles). There is one tunnel — Schwanden (66.75m; 219ft) — and seven bridges of 97m (318ft) total length. Station altitudes are as follows: Vitznau 439m (1,440ft) above sea level; Rigi Kaltbad 1,453m (4,767ft); and Rigi Kulm 1,755m (5,758ft). The present travelling time is 35min, with electric traction vehicles running uphill at 11.2mph and 7.5mph downhill. The VRB is more convenient for passengers from the Luzern direction, whereas the ARB caters more for people from the Zürich area. The two lines merged in 1992 and became the Rigibahnen; however, the ex-VRB retains its red livery, whilst the ex-ARB maintains its blue colours.

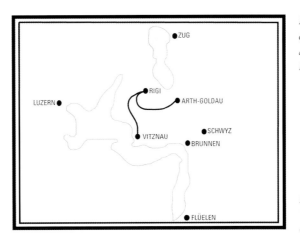

Map showing the location of the Vitznau-Rigi Railway and the Arth-Goldau-Rigi Railway.

At Kräbel station on the ARB there is a cableway to Rigi-Scheidegg run by the RSAG. It is 1.8km (1.18 miles) in length and the height difference is 880m (2,887ft). It is intended that the RB and the RSAG will amalgamate during 2013, which would then make it possible for passengers to make a round trip on the Rigi by using both railway lines, the cableway and walking the trackbed of the closed Scheideggbahn.

Below: The base station at Vitznau on 11 June 1956. Class Bhe2/4 No 2, built by SLM/BBC in 1937, and Class H1/2 No 7, built by SLM in 1873, on a plinth demonstrate two generations of the line's motive power. Between the two is a stone memorial to Niklaus Riggenbach.

A close-up of preserved Class H1/2 No 7 of 1873 and the memorial to Niklaus Riggenbach (1817-1899) at the base station, on 11 June 1956. No 7 is, at the time of writing, in the transport museum at Luzern.

VRB Class Bhe2/4 No 3, built by SLM/BBC in 1937, at Rigi Staffel on 11 June 1956. The Arth-Goldau Bahn (ARB) joins the Vitznau line here and runs parallel to the summit at Rigi Kulm.

VRB Class Bhe2/4 No 3 stands with a trailer at Rigi Kulm on 11 June 1956.

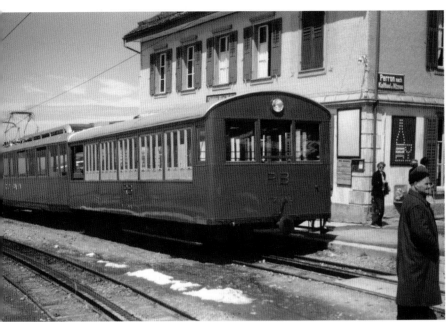

The pristine trailer attached to No 3 at Rigi Kulm on 11 June 1956.

*The later type Gleichstrom-Zahnradtriebwagen, VRB Class Bhe4/4
No 31 and trailer pose for an official photograph. VRB*

*A facsimile of a postcard promoting the Arth-Goldau Bahn, dating
originally to circa 1910. Biregg Verlag AG CH-6003, Luzern*

*An advert issued by
Société Anonyme des
Ateliers de Sécheron
(SAAS), Geneva,
detailing the railcars
supplied to the line from
the late 1940s onwards.
Author's collection*

ARB Class BDhe2/4 No 13, built by SLM/SAAS in 1954 (Works No 4121), is arriving at Rigi Kulm on 11 June 1956.

A later type Gleichstrom-Zahnradtriebwagen ARB Class Bhe4/4, No 25, and trailer at the Rigi-Scheidegg cableway terminus. ARB

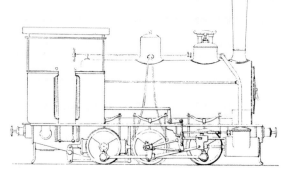

The Rigi-Scheideggbahn opened with three adhesion Class C3/3 0-6-0T locomotives, Nos 1-3, built by SLM in 1874 (Works Nos 32, 34 and 37). These were purchased at a cost of SFr 35,000 each. SLM

RIGI-SCHEIDEGGBAHN

This metre-gauge line diverged from the Vitznau-Rigi Bahn at Kaltbad and ran 6.4km (4 miles) along the crest of the ridge to Scheidegg. It opened from Kaltbad to Unterstetten on 14 July 1874, and from Unterstetten to Scheidegg on 1 July 1875. The line was steam worked throughout its existence, closing on 21 September 1931. After official closure, it was operated occasionally by an hotelier in 1933, and again at various times until 1942. All that now remains are the formation and trackbed.

The Scheideggstrasse is now a footpath but was once the trackbed of the Rigi-Scheideggbahn. This is how it looked on 11 June 1956. The author's parents were great walkers and his mother is shown here in the background.

THE ROUTE OF THE
GLACIER EXPRESS

BRIG-VISP-ZERMATT BAHN (BVZ)

AT Visp on the SBB main line the metre-gauge Abt rack/adhesion line to Zermatt was opened in stages: from Visp to Stalden on 3 July 1890; from Stalden to St Niklaus on 26 August 1890; and from St Niklaus to Zermatt on 18 July 1891. The line was first operated by steam and was originally known as the Compagnie du Chemin de Fer de Viège à Zermatt SA. It was managed by the Jura-Simplon Bahn, before passing to the SBB/CFF in 1903. It then regulated itself from 1927 as the BVZ. On 1 October 1929, the line was electrified from Visp to Zermatt, and a new electrified metre-gauge line parallel with the SBB was opened on 5 June 1930 from Visp to Brig to allow connection to be made with the Furka-Oberalp Bahn.

The BVZ was the first private railway in Switzerland to adopt the automatic block system throughout. The 44km (27-mile) line, which rises 955m (3,133ft), operates on 11kV 16.7Hz ac. At the time of writing, there are no road vehicles allowed into Zermatt, except those that are specially authorised. At Täsch, which is about 6km from Zermatt, there is a large car park where passengers can travel forward on a shuttle service; this also conveys a luggage van in the summer months. In 2003, this line merged with the Furka-Oberalp Bahn and became the Matterhorn Gotthard Bahn (MGB).

Continued on page 162

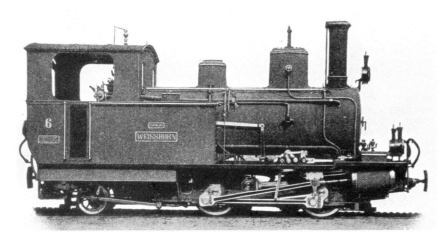

Above and below: Eight Class C2/3 0-4-2T rack/adhesion locomotives were supplied by SLM to the BVZ: No 1 Matterhorn, built in 1890 (Works No 609); No 2 Monte Rosa (610 of 1890); No 3 Mischabel (611 of 1890); No 4 Gornergrat (612 of 1890); No 5 St Theodule (796 of 1893); No 6 Weisshorn (1410 of 1902); No 7 Breithorn (1725 of 1906); and No 8 Lyskamm (1947 of 1908). All were withdrawn in 1922. Author's collection

7245   Chemin de fer Viège-Zermatt et la Viège (Vispbach)

Above: A very scenic view of the Vispertal (Viège Valley) on the BVZ, produced circa 1900, showing a typical steam-hauled Visp-Zermatt train. Phototypie Co, Neuchâtel

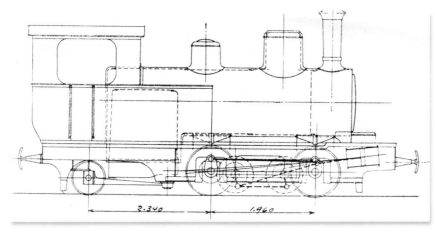

2.340   1.960

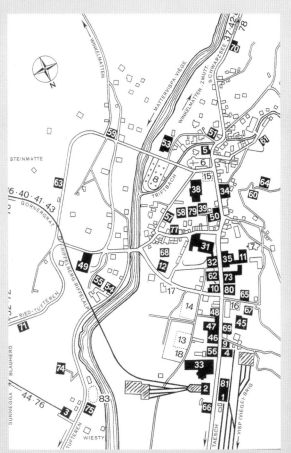

A plan of Zermatt, showing
the main BVZ (MGB)
station (1). The other station
at right angles is the base
station of the Gornergratbahn
(GGB).

BVZ Class HGe4/4 No 13, built by SLM/SWS/MFO in 1929, arrives at Zermatt on
22 May 1957.

A view of Zermatt, showing both stations, taken from the slopes above the town on 22 May 1957.

BVZ Class HGe4/4 No 13 on the 'Glacier Express' at Zermatt on 3 June 1957. The locomotive is able to work on both rack and adhesion sections. The coaches would have worked through to St Moritz via the Furka-Oberalp Bahn and the Rhätische Bahn.

A close-up of BVZ AB4/ü coach No 161 on 3 June 1957 shows the destination board at Zermatt. The initials 'F O' are those of the Furka-Oberalp Bahn and nothing more sinister!

Furka-Oberalp Bahn Class HGe4/4 No 33, built by SLM in 1940 (Works No 3725), on shed at Zermatt on 23 May 1957. Furka-Oberalp locomotives regularly worked through on to the BVZ.

Furka-Oberalp Bahn Class HGe4/4 No 33 leaves Zermatt with a mixed train on 23 May 1957. One wonders whether the last vehicle could be used as fourth class!

158

BVZ Class HGe4/4 No 14, built by SLM/SWS/MFO in 1929, on shed at Zermatt on 26 May 1957.
These locomotives in their very bright red livery look almost like fire engines.

The magnificent Matterhorn taken from a lane at Zermatt on 21 May 1957. The summit of this mighty peak is 4,504m (14,780ft) above sea level and was first ascended, by a party of four Englishmen and three guides led by Edward Whymper (1840-1911), on 14 July 1865. On the descent, however, three tourists and a guide fell onto the glacier below and perished. Whymper was one of the survivors.

A view of the BVZ line and valley with the village of Täsch in the background on 25 May 1957. The village and the railway were partly washed away by an avalanche in 1958, but the Swiss soon had everything up and running again.

The BVZ/FO line carries a considerable amount of freight and supplies. A typical four-wheel wagon, No 901, is loaded with building material for the construction of the new cableway to Schwarzsee when seen at Zermatt on 1 June 1957. Note that the wagon is equipped with the appropriate gear-wheel on one axle for use on the rack sections.

ZERMATT

LUFTSEILBAHN ZERMATT-SCHWARZSEE (LZS)

Whilst the author was in Zermatt in 1957, the construction of this cableway was ongoing. It now runs from Zermatt — 1,605m (5,265ft) above sea level — to Schwarzsee at 2,584m (8,480ft), which is a further step to reach the slopes of the Matterhorn itself. There are plans to go even higher.

On 30 May 1957, trial running was taking place and car No 2 is seen on the ascent with a wooden crate carrying dynamite for further blasting operations at the summit station.

No 2 is seen again with a further supply of crates destined for the top station, on 30 May 1957.

The base station still under construction on 30 May 1957.

The author managed to obtain a ride on both cars on 30 May 1957. No worries about Health & Safety; my permit again proved very useful. Car No 1 is seen in a view taken from No 2.

The brochure shows the route of the GGB plus one of the Rowan units, whilst the map shows the route of the line from Zermatt to Gornergrat. It is amazing that heights and mileages published in official documents vary enormously, particularly concerning the height of the Matterhorn! GGB AG

GORNERGRATBAHN (GGB)

At right angles to the main BVZ/MGB station at Zermatt is the terminus of the Gornergratbahn; this line is metre gauge and rack operated throughout on the Abt system. It was electric powered from its opening on 20 August 1898, but did have one steam locomotive — 0-4-2T No 8, built in 1892 (Works No 748). This may possibly have been used during construction, being retained as reserve power. Remembering that the Gornergratbahn started off electric powered and perhaps problems could have been expected, it would make sense to have a steam locomotive in reserve. A higher station at Gornergrat Kulm was opened on 1 June 1909, which made it the highest open-air station in Europe at 3,089m (10,134ft). The line operates at 725V, 50Hz, three-phase and is 9.33km (5.8 miles) long. The line climbs at a 1 in 5 (20%) maximum gradient through 1,484m (4,869ft) to Gornergrat Kulm. The main intermediate stops are at Riffelalp 2,210m (7,250ft); Riffelberg 2,582m (8,471ft); and Rotenboden 2,819m (9,248ft). At Riffelalp there was a short tramway running to a hotel that burnt down in 1960, after which the tramway closed.

11168 - Chemin de fer du Gornergrat
Station Riffelberg (2585 m) et le Cervin (Matterhorn) 4505 m

A view from the cab of GGB No 103 shows the complexity of an Abt rack point at a passing loop, on 23 May 1957.

Above: A view of Riffelberg station showing a Rowan unit on the way to the summit in a postcard produced circa 1900. Phototypie Co, Neuchâtel

GGB Class Bhe2/4 No 103, built by SLM/BBC in 1952 (Works No 4076), runs into the base station at Zermatt on 23 May 1957. Note the twin pantographs needed because the system is three-phase and requires two overhead wires. This line and the Jungfraubahn are the only two lines using this system. These railcars are now numbered in the 3000 series.

Another view from the cab of No 103 shows the track and Abt rack plus the approaching tunnel, on 23 May 1957.

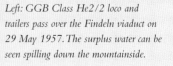

Above: GGB Class Bhe2/4 No 104, built by SLM/BBC in 1952 (Works No 4077), crosses Findeln viaduct on 22 May 1957. The Gornergratbahn has its own hydroelectric power station, and the surplus water was discharged down the mountainside. Though on this occasion there was no surplus water as more power was needed.

Left: GGB Class He2/2 loco and trailers pass over the Findeln viaduct on 29 May 1957. The surplus water can be seen spilling down the mountainside.

A GGB Works train hauled by Class He2/2 No 4, built by SLM in 1902 (Works No 1437), crosses Findeln viaduct on 27 May 1957.

GGB Rowan unit No 1, built by SLM in 1897 (Works No 1065), is seen with a loaded wagon in a siding at Gornergrat Kulm on 23 May 1957.

GGB Class Bhe2/4 No 104 at Gornergrat Kulm on 23 May 1957.

GGB Class He2/2 No 4 with its original bow collectors at Zermatt on 23 May 1957.

The Matterhorn from the GGB's summit station on 23 May 1957. Note the bag on a seat in the deep snow.

167

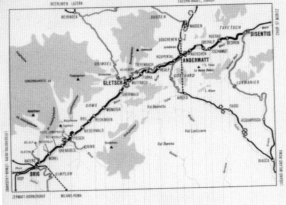

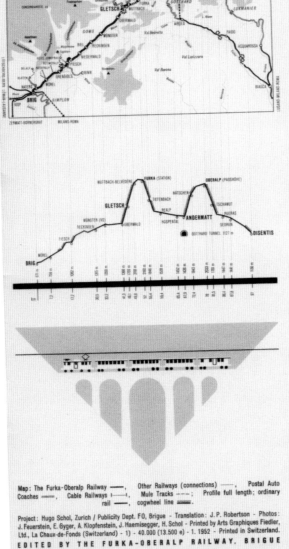

The cover of a 1952 Furka-Oberalp Bahn brochure, showing the line and gradients. Furka–Oberalp Bahn

FURKA-OBERALP BAHN (FO)

A metre-gauge line providing access to the Swiss Alps between the Cantons of Wallis and Graubünden in an east–west direction, the Furka-Oberalp Bahn linked the Rhine and Rhône valleys by way of an extremely steep climb over the Furka and Oberalp passes achieved with the help of a number of Abt rack sections. Approximately 97m (60 miles) in length, the line climbs 1,489m (4,887ft) between Brig and Furka over maximum gradients of 1 in 9 (11%). Between Furka and Andermatt is a fall of 709.5m (2,328ft), before starting a climb up to Oberalppasshöhe of 597m (1,960ft), then a final descent of 903m (2,964ft) to Disentis. Connection is made with the Rhätische Bahn at Disentis/Mustér.

The railway was originally entitled the Compagnie Suisse du Chemin de Fer de la Furka and was set up in 1910. It became the Furka-Oberalp Bahn in 1926. The line was opened in stages, from Brig to Oberwald on 1 June 1915; Oberwald to Gletsch on 1 July 1916; and Gletsch to Disentis on 4 July 1926. It was electrified between 5 July 1940 and 1 July 1942, using the same voltage as the BVZ. At Andermatt there is a short metre-gauge Abt rack link line to Göschenen on the Gotthard line, known as the Schöllenenbahn, which opened on 12 July 1917; it was taken over by the Furka-Oberalp Bahn in 1960. Until the 15km (9½-mile) Furka base tunnel between Realp and Oberwald was opened in 1982, the FO had to be worked in two sections during the winter months when the mountain passes were closed. It was only when the tunnel link opened that all-year-round operation became possible. The old route passing by the Rhône glacier is now a preserved line — the Dampfbahn Furka-Bergstrecke (DFB) — using steam locomotives and is a great attraction. On 1 January 2003, the Furka-Oberalp Bahn merged with the Brig-Visp-Zermatt Bahn to become the MGB.

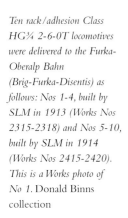

Ten rack/adhesion Class HG¾ 2-6-0T locomotives were delivered to the Furka-Oberalp Bahn (Brig-Furka-Disentis) as follows: Nos 1-4, built by SLM in 1913 (Works Nos 2315-2318) and Nos 5-10, built by SLM in 1914 (Works Nos 2415-2420). This is a Works photo of No 1. Donald Binns collection

A view of the preserved DFB No 3, taken by the author at the Chemin de Fer de la Baie de Somme Railway's open day on 26 April 2009. No 3 is normally based at the Blonay-Chamby Museum Railway. Others of the class finished up in Vietnam but came back and are now operating on the Dampfbahn Furka-Bergstrecke line. The privately preserved DFB opened throughout to Oberwald on 12 August 2010, with the first service being worked by DFB No 1.

A close-up of a standard SLM Works plate; this is from the preserved DFB No 3 as seen in France on 26 April 2009.

After the electrification of the Disentis-Andermatt section of the FO in 1940, four Class HGe4/4 locomotives were purchased from SLM. These became Nos 31-34 and had an adhesion top speed of 34mph and a rack speed of 18.6mph. Following completion of electrification, further locomotives — Nos 35 and 36 — arrived, with a seventh (No 37) arriving in 1956. All were basically similar except that No 37 had welded instead of riveted sides. A colour shot of No 33, at Zermatt, appears on page 158, but here is a further view of the same locomotive, again on 23 May 1957.

Two MGB push-pull units pass between Disentis and Andermatt on 27 June 2008. The locomotive on the other end of the approaching train is Class Deh4/4 No 95 Andermatt.

The view of the MGB's Andermatt station taken from a descending train on 27 June 2008. The line going to the right in the picture is to Disentis, and the line in the foreground at the bottom of the picture is the Schöllenenbahn link to Göschenen.

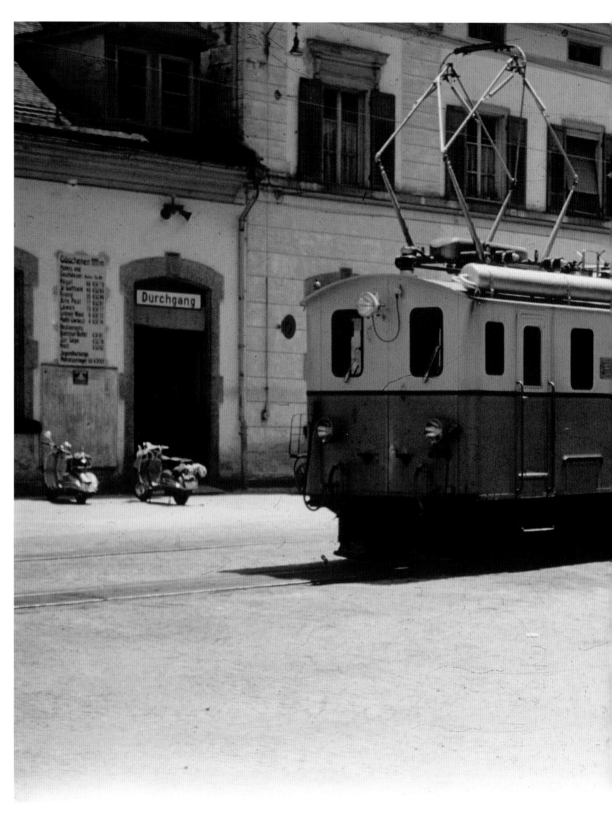

SchB Class He2/2 No 1,
built by SLM in 1915
(Works No 2465),
at Göschenen on
18 June 1958.

SCHÖLLENENBAHN (SchB)

This line is 5.63km (3½ miles) in length and links the MGB at Andermatt with the Gotthard Railway at Göschenen. It has a maximum gradient of 1 in 5½ (18%) with a height difference between its two terminals of 329m (1,081ft). The line originally ran on 1,200V dc, but was converted to the Furka-Oberalp standard of 11kV 16.7Hz ac in 1941. It became part of the FO system in 1960, and is now fully integrated into the MGB.

An undated but pre-World War 2 view of the approaches to Göschenen. On the left an SBB train leaves the northern portal of the Gotthard Tunnel, whilst on the right a Schöllenenbahn train ascends the rack line to Andermatt.
Railway Gazette

A view of the magnificent Matterhorn taken from a very muddy lane near Zermatt on 22 May 1957.

The main street in Zermatt on 22 May 1957 with the author's parents enjoying breakfast at the Hotel Pollux.

CHUR, RHÄTISCHE BAHN AND ST MORITZ-DORF

CHUR BAHNHOF SBB/RhB

THE line from Rorschach to Rheineck was opened by the Vereinigte Schweizerbahnen on 25 August 1857, and from Rheineck to Chur by the same company on 1 July 1858. Chur station was originally opened in 1860, and was added to in 1861; further work was undertaken in 1876. A new station was constructed and opened in 1878. With the arrival of the Rhätische Bahn in 1896, the station was extended between then and 1898, and an administrative block for the Rhätische Bahn was added in 1899. Further trackwork was installed in 1903. A new buffet was provided in 1907, and other work was carried out in 1922 and 1928.

One of the SBB IC 2000 second-class double-deck coaches stands in the platform at Chur on 26 June 2008.

SBB Class Re460 No 460 020-1, officially named SBB Locomotive Drivers, although the name was not carried as the locomotive is in advertising livery, awaits departure from Chur on 25 June 2008. The author's very good friend John Goodman, 93 years old in 2013, makes his way up the platform.

SBB Class Re4/4^{II} No 11147 at Chur on 25 June 2008.

RHÄTISCHE BAHN

In south-eastern Switzerland is the Graubünden or Grison region where one encounters the Rhätische Bahn, a metre-gauge adhesion network administered from Chur. Its main line is linked to the Furka-Oberalp Bahn at Disentis and via this line at Brig to the Brig-Visp-Zermatt. Through trains, including the 'Glacier Express', run between St Moritz, Chur and Zermatt. The Rhätische Bahn is the largest independent railway in Switzerland, construction commencing on 29 June 1888. The first trains ran between Landquart and Klosters on 9 October 1889 over what was then called the 'Landquart-Davos Narrow Gauge Railway'. The next 16km (10 miles) to Davos opened on 21 July 1890.

The line was successful from the start, and other railway projects came into being; in 1894, work commenced on an extension from Landquart to Chur, then on to Thusis. A new name — Rhätische Bahn AG — was adopted in 1894. The Rhätische Bahn opened in sections:

The Davos line:
Landquart-Klosters
    Opened 9 October 1889
    Electrified 7 November 1921
Klosters-Davos
    Opened 21 July 1890
    Electrified 1 December 1920
Davos-Filisur
    Opened 1 July 1909
    Electrified 11 December 1919
Landquart-Filisur 43 miles long; maximum gradient
    1 in 22 (5%)
    Electrified at 11kV, 16²/₃Hz ac
    20 tunnels total length 7km (4.4 miles)
    88 bridges with a total length of 1.83km
    (1.14 miles)
    Climbs 1,033m (3,390ft) from Landquart to
    Davos then descends 478.5m (1,570ft) to Filisur.

The Albula line:
Chur-Thusis
    Opened 1 July 1896
    Electrified 7 November 1921
Landquart-Chur
    Opened 29 August 1896
    Electrified 7 November 1921
Reichenau-Trin
    Opened 1 June 1903
    Electrified 7 November 1921
Trin-Ilanz
    Opened 1 June 1903
    Electrified 17 May 1922
Thusis-Celerina
    Opened 1 July 1903
    Electrified 2 April 1919
Celerina-St Moritz
    Opened 10 July 1904

Electrified 1 July 1913
Total length of route is 103km (64 miles);
maximum gradient 1 in 22 (5%)
Climbs 4,240ft between Landquart and the
Albula Tunnel and then falls 39.6m (130ft) to
St Moritz
Electrified at 11kV, 16²/₃Hz ac.

There are many well-known engineering works on this line: Soliser viaduct (90m; 295ft high); the 130m (426ft)-long curved Landwasser viaduct (94m [309ft] radius, 65m [213ft] high and on a 1 in 50 gradient); between Bergün and Preda there are no fewer than six hairpins and the Albula Tunnel (between Preda and Spinas); 5.8km (3.6 miles) long at 1,829m (6,000ft) above sea level; there are 41 other tunnels with a total length of 10.62km (6.6 miles), along with 152 bridges, totalling 3.43km (2.14km).

The Surselva line:
    Starts at Reichenau on the Albula line. Work started in
    1900 and Ilanz, the first town on the Rhine, was reached
    in 1910. The whole line — Ilanz to Disentis — opened on
    3 August 1912
    Electrified on 17 May 1922 at 11kV, 16²/₃Hz ac
    The line's length is 48.2km (30 miles) and includes six
    tunnels (totalling 1.28km [0.8 miles]) and 63 bridges
    (totalling 2.67km [1.65 miles])
    Climbs 521m (1,710ft) from Reichenau to Disentis.

The Engadin line:
    After four years' construction, the Engadin line from
    Bever to Scuol (Schuls) near the Austrian border
    opened on 1 July 1913
    Electrified from the start at 11kV, 16²/₃Hz ac
    The route is 50km (31 miles) in length and includes 17
    tunnels (totalling 8.04km (eight miles) and 73 bridges
    (totalling 2.25km [1.4 miles])
    The maximum gradient is 1 in 40 and the line falls
    426.7km (1,400ft) to Scuol-Tarasp.

The Arosa line:
    The railway between Chur and Arosa opened on
    12 December 1914 and was built by a separate
    company; it was taken over by the RhB in 1942
    Electrified from opening at 2,400V dc and converted to
    11kV, 16²/₃Hz ac in 1997 Adhesion throughout, there is a
    maximum gradient of 1 in 17 and a climb of 1,152m
    (3,780ft) to Arosa.

Berninabahn:
    When the RhB reached St Moritz it was logical to extend
    southwards by way of the Bernina Pass into Italy.
    Accordingly, construction of the Berninabahn
    commenced in 1906 and the line opened to Tirano on
    5 July 1910. The Berninabahn was acquired by the RhB
    in 1943, although the track in Italy — from

Campocologno to Tirano — was at first only leased
Electrified from the start at 750V dc, the installation was
later altered to 1,000V dc
This is a difficult line with 1 in 14 adhesion gradients
climbing 3,760ft from Samedan to Bernina Ospizio and
then descending 1,829m (6,000ft) to Tirano. The line's

highest point — the Bernina Pass — lies at 2,256m
(7,400ft) above sea level. The line is 66km (41) miles in
length with 13 tunnels (totalling 4km [2.5 miles]) and 55
bridges (totalling 816m [2,676ft]).

Continued on page 194

Map of the Rhätische Bahn (left) with detailed map of the northern approaches to the Albula Tunnel (right).
Railway Gazette

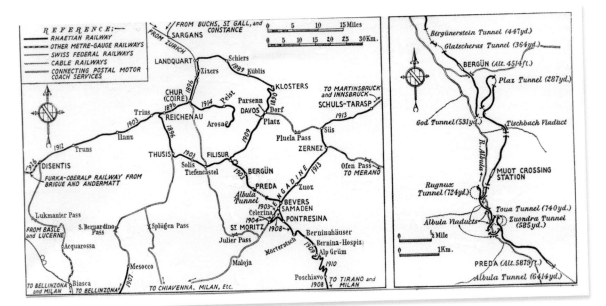

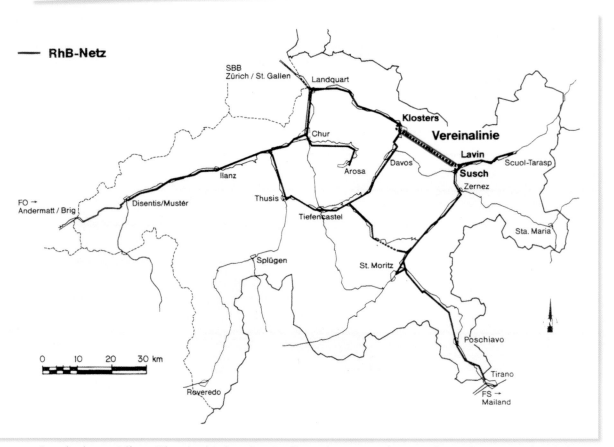

A new line between Selfranga (Klosters) and Sagliains (Süss/Susch) opened on 22 November 1999. There are three new tunnels on the line: the Vereina 19.05km (12 miles); the Zugweld 2.17km (1.4 miles); and the short Susch 0.3km (984ft). Construction of the Vereina Tunnel was the major undertaking on the route and, after years of work, the breakthrough came about on 26 March 1997. This route has speeded up travel considerably, and there is also a 'Motorail' service through the tunnel. RhB/SRS

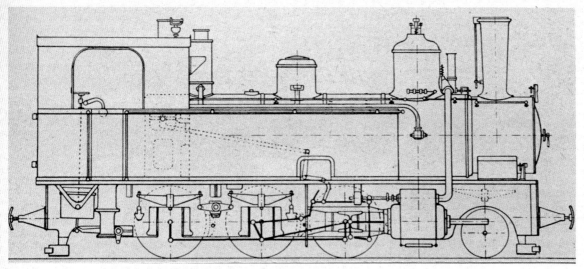

Above: Sixteen 2-6-0T locomotives for adhesion working were purchased by the Landquart-Davos company in three batches from SLM. The first batch of five were for use between Landquart and Davos:

Number	Name	Works No	Year
1	Rhatia	577	1889
2	Prätigau	578	1889
3	Davos	579	1889
4	Flüela	580	1889
5	Engadin	581	1889

The second batch comprised three locomotives and were purchased by the RhB for the opening of the Landquart-Chur-Thusis line:

6	Landquart	960	1896
7	Chur	961	1896
8	Thusis	962	1896

The final batch of eight were larger and more power locomotives: Nos 9/10 (Works Nos 1369/70) of 1901; Nos 11-14 (Works Nos 1476-1479) of 1903; and Nos 15/16 (Works Nos 1910/11) of 1908. Donald Binns collection

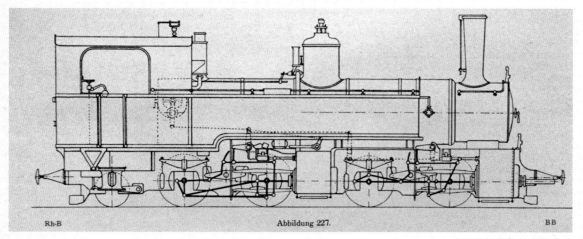

Rh-B   Abbildung 227.   BB

Above and left: A pair of Mallet G2/2+2/3 0-4-4-2T locomotives were built by SLM for the RhB in 1896 — Nos 23 and 24 (Works Nos 958-9) — for the opening of the Landquart-Chur-Thusis line. Their names were Maloja *and* Chiavenna *respectively. SLM*

SLM-Winterthur

A final batch of eight Mallet G2/3+2/2 semi-articulated locomotives for the RhB were supplied by SLM: Nos 25-29 (Works Nos 1480-1484) in 1902, and Nos 30-32 (Works Nos 1485-1487) in 1903. These were for use on the Albula line. When the line was electrified Nos 25, 29, 30 plus possibly No 32 were sold to Madagascar in January 1921; they were scrapped in 1951. In 1947, Nos 26 and 28 were sold to a Spanish mine and then to another concern in Spain. No 26 was scrapped after 1961, and No 28 after 1969. No 27 was sold in 1921 to the Yverdon Ste-Croix railway and survived until 1946. SLM

The south-eastern terminus of the 'Glacier Express' is St Moritz, seen here at 12.10pm on 3 June 1956. No parked cars to spoil the view — excellent!

RhB Class Ge4/4 No 601 Albula, built by SLM in 1947 (Works No 3921; BBC Works No 4544), stands in the platform at St Moritz on the 10.18am train to Chur on 3 June 1956.

A change in the weather: 18in of snow overnight, but the 10.18am train to Chur still departed on time from St Moritz on 8 June 1956. No 'wrong type of snow' on the Rhätische Bahn. Class Ge4/4 No 603 Badus, built by SLM in 1947 (Works No 3922; BBC Works No 4545), provides the motive power on this occasion. This class has since been rebuilt with new cabs and fitted for push-pull operation.

*A 'summer' morning in
St Moritz on 8 June 1956!*

*RhB Class Ge4/4 No 603
Badus shunts a Speisewagen
(Restaurant Car) at
St Moritz on 8 June 1956.
This vehicle became part of
the 10.18am train to Chur.*

RhB Class Ge4/6 No 391, built by SLM/AEG in 1913, hauls a freight through St Moritz on 9 June 1956. This locomotive had widely spaced pairs of coupled driving axles driven by a crankshaft between them. A pair of connecting rods through the floor came from another crankshaft that was driven by step-down gearing from two high-speed motors. The electrical gear was supplied by AEG of Berlin. No 391 was withdrawn in 1974; it was preserved by the Deutsche Gesellschaft für Eisenbahngeschichte (DGEG) in Berlin in 1980.

A roadside view of Scuol-Tarasp station on 6 June 1956. The architecture is typical of the Graubünden region. When this line opened, on 1 July 1913, the intention was that it should join the Arlberg line near Landeck, but this was not pursued because of the outbreak of World War 1 the following year.

RhB Triebwagen ABe4/4
No 502, built by
SWS/BBC/MFO in
1939, is seen at Scuol-Tarasp
on 6 June 1956. At this time
these units were used on this
line and between Samedan
and Pontresina.

17729   Berninabahn und Palügletscher

The cobbled streets and ancient buildings of Scuol (Schuls) village on
6 June1956. Well worth a visit.

This commercial postcard shows an early Triebwagen and two trailers,
in original yellow livery, passing the Palù glacier very soon after the
opening of the line on 5 July 1910. Wehrli-Verlag Kilchberg,
Zürich

RhB Triebwagen Class ABe4/4 No 37, built by SIG/SAAS/MFO in 1909 and rebuilt during 1949-51, hauls a freight wagon near St Moritz on 8 June 1956.

RhB No 37 is on a mixed train at Morteratsch on 4 June 1956. Note that the railcar has both a normal pantograph and a bow collector.

RhB Triebwagen Class BCe4/4 No 6, built circa 1909, seen in use as a service vehicle, sporting original livery at Morteratsch on 5 June 1956. Note the two bow collectors.

The RhB's Ospizio Bernina station is situated 2,256m (7,403ft) above sea level between Alp Grüm and Pontresina and is seen here on 5 June 1957. Note the vitreous enamel signs, the antiquated station furniture, milk churns and block bells. The station was definitely built to withstand very adverse weather conditions. A senior member of the station staff is ready to give the 'right away' on the right.

A summer view of Lake Bianco taken from the RhB train, near Ospizio Bernina, on 5 June 1956.

Alp Grüm station (2,090m [6,960ft] above sea level) with RhB Triebwagen Class ABe4/4 No 3 in use as a service vehicle hauling a freight wagon, on 5 June 1956. This time the Triebwagen is in green and white livery.

Just after Alp Grüm, the RhB line descends southwards into the Cavaglia Valley by spirals to Poschiavo (1,013m [3,325ft] above sea level) and then on to Tirano (Italy). This shows the view in question on 5 June 1956.

Alp Grüm pictured 52 years later on 26 June 2008 showing RhB Class Abe4/4 Nos 49 and 48, which were built by SWS/BBC/SAAS in 1972, on a train bound for Tirano.

A view from the RhB train on the journey from St Moritz to Chur, near Preda on 10 June 1956. The service was hauled by Class Ge4/4 No 601 Albula.

RhB Class Ge4/4^{III} No 642 Breil/Brigels, built by SLM/ABB in 1993, at Samedan on 27 August 2003, advertising 100 years of the Albula and Ruinaulta line. John Goodman

Above: A commercial postcard dating to circa 1910 shows the RhB's Landwasser viaduct with a train prior to electrification. Gebr. Wehrli, Kilchberg, Zürich

RhB Class Ge4/4^III No 652 Vaz/Obervaz Lenzerheide-Valbella, *built by SLM/ABB in 1997, leaves the tunnel and crosses the Landwasser viaduct near Filisur on 27 June 2003.* John Goodman

RhB Class Ge4/4^II No 611 Landquart, *built by SLM/BBC in 1973, heads a train leaving the tunnel and onto the Landwasser viaduct on 26 June 2003.* John Goodman

*RhB Class Ge4/4^{III}
No 642 appears again, this
time on a train bound for
Chur leaving the Landwasser
viaduct on 26 June 2008.*

*RhB Class Ge4/4^{II}
No 614* Schiers, *built by
SLM/BBC in 1973, and
Ge4/4^{III} No 641*
Maienfeld, *supplied by the
same manufacturers in 1993,
stand in adjacent platforms at
Chur on 24 June 2008.
The latter sports an
advertising livery.*

*RhB Class Ge4/4^{II}
No 616* Filisur, *built by
SLM/BBC in 1973, and
Class Ge4/4^{III} No 651*
Fideris *await departure at
Chur on 26 June 2008.
No 651 was in a livery
advertising the 'Glacier
Express'.*

RhB Class Ge6/6 No 706
Disentis/Mustér, *supplied*
by SLM/BBC/MFO in
1965, waits to depart with a
freight train at Reichenau on
25 June 2008. This class of
locomotive is articulated and
is used mainly on freight
services.

RhB Class Tmf2/2
No 120, a diesel shunter
built in 2004 by
SCHÖMA of Diepholz,
Germany, is seen at
Reichenau on 25 June
2008.

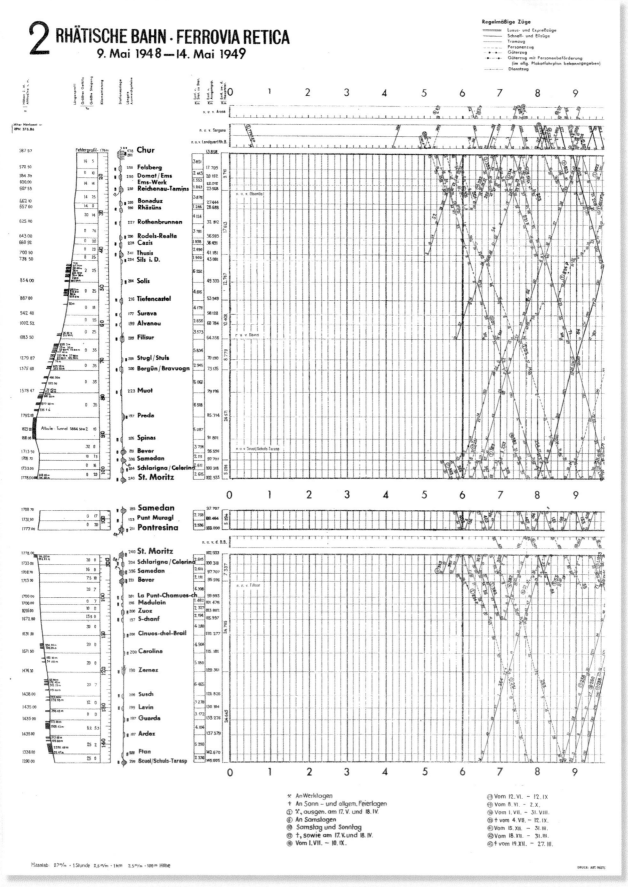

A section of the working timetable covering the period 9 May 1948 to 14 May 1949. RhB

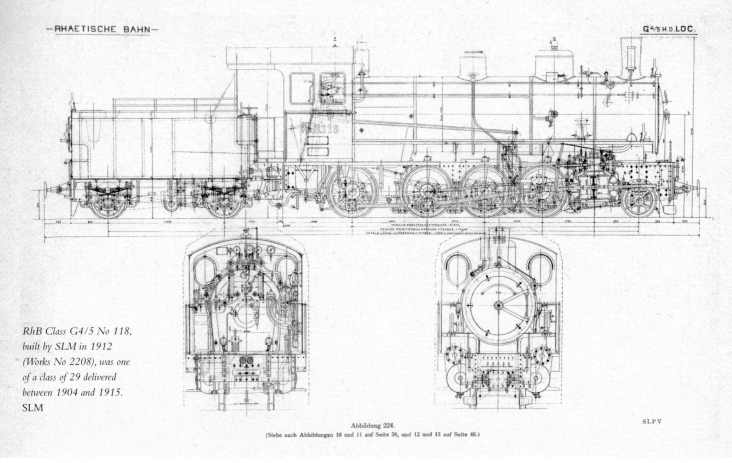

-RHAETISCHE BAHN-

G4/5 H.D. LOC.

RhB Class G4/5 No 118, built by SLM in 1912 (Works No 2208), was one of a class of 29 delivered between 1904 and 1915. SLM

Abbildung 224.
(Siehe auch Abbildungen 10 und 11 auf Seite 38, und 12 und 13 auf Seite 46.)

SLPV

ST MORITZ-DORF

At St Moritz, 1,821m (5,975ft) above sea level, one can get to the summit of the Piz Nair, 3,052m (10,000ft) above sea level, by means of two funiculars and then by cable car. The first stage is from St Moritz to Chanterella at 2,005m (6,578ft), then Chanterella to Corviglia (2,490m [8,169ft]), and lastly from Corviglia to Piz Nair. The metre-gauge St Moritz-Chanterella section, opened on 2 January 1913, is 451m (1,480ft) in length and has a total ascent of 162m (531ft). The 800mm-gauge second stage from Chanterella to Corviglia, opened on 19 December 1928, is 1630m (5349ft) in length and has a total ascent of 480m (1,575ft). The section between Chanterella and Corviglia was brought up to date in 1985 when the track was changed to standard gauge and new railcars were introduced. The stage from St Moritz to Chanterella was modernised in 1994 with new railcars and the track changed from metre gauge to 1,150mm.

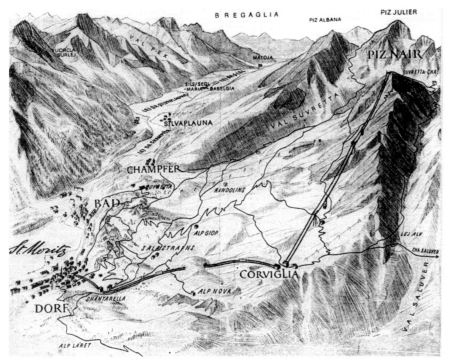

Map of the St Moritz-Dorf region, showing the two funiculars and the cable car.

Below: St Moritz-Chanterella Bahn car No 1 on the lower end of the line, on 5 June 1956.

The second stage Corviglia Bahn car No 1, built by Autokasten München in November 1928, pictured on 5 June 1956.

A view of the ascent from the Corviglia Bahn, showing St Moritz in the distance on 5 June 1956.

The lower station of the Corviglia-Piz Nair cableway seen on 5 June 1956, not long after the line had opened.

Car No 1 of the Corviglia-Piz Nair cableway, photographed from No 2 on 5 June 1956.

Car No 2 of the Corviglia-Piz Nair cableway, photographed from No 1 on 5 June 1956.
These last two illustrations give some idea of the very powerful scenery on this particular trip.

Far right: A close-up of the very intricate running gear using two cables on the Corviglia-Piz
Nair cableway.

RORSCHACH HEIDEN BERGBAHN; SCHWEIZERISCHE-ALPENPOSTEN; VERKEHRSBETRIEBE DER STADT ZÜRICH; BASEL

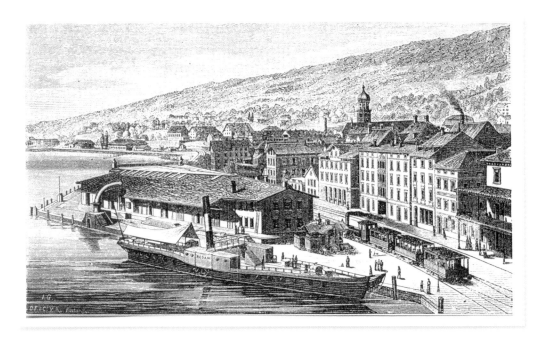

An engraving depicting the Rorschach Heiden Bergbahn at Rorschach (from Heiden und die Rorschach Heiden Bahn by H. Szadrowsky, published by Orell Füssli & Co, Zürich, circa 1880).
Author's collection

RORSCHACH HEIDEN BERGBAHN (RHB)

FOLLOWING the success of Riggenbach with climbing the Rigi, it was decided to build a similar type of mountain railway to the heights of Heiden from the shores of the Bodensee (Lake Constance). The Rorschach Heiden Bahn was built under the direction of engineer Otto Drossel, using the Riggenbach rack system as on the Vitznau-Rigi Bahn. The line opened on 6 September 1875 and cost SFr 2.2 million to construct. Steam locomotives Nos 1-3 were built at Aarau (Works Nos 6, 7 and 8) and No 4 was built at Winterthur (Works No 1287). The line was electrified on 15 May 1930; the present voltage is 15kV 16.7Hz ac. The railway was built to standard gauge and the length of the line is 5.63km (3½ miles) with an ascent of 395m (1,296ft), the average gradient being 1 in 11 (9%) with a curve radius of 80m (262.5ft). Heiden lies at 806m (2,645ft) above sea level and 412m (1,352ft) above the Bodensee. The line started from the harbour station at Rorschach, climbing initially at 1 in 14, then 1 in 11. On the night of 23 October 1875, shortly after opening, the line was destroyed by a mountain landside at Krähenwald, causing much damage.

From Heiden it is possible to see the town of Friedrichshafen in Germany across the lake; this was the

The RHB station at Wienacht, 2.41km (1½ miles) from Rorschach (also from Heiden und die Rorschach Heiden Bahn). Author's collection

Above: A drawing and photograph of RHB locomotives Nos 1-4. SLM

*RHB ABDeh2/4 No 23,
built by SLM/BBC/FFA
in 1953, at Heiden on
26 Sept 1995, with the
08.52 to Rorschach Hafen.
John Armitstead*

*The BT line from
St Gallen to Rorschach
(Hafen) was opened by
the St Gallisch Appenzell
Bahn on 25 October 1856.
Later the line became part of
the Bodensee-Toggenburg
Bahn (BT) and now is under
the control of the Südostbahn
(SOB). The postcard shows
the new station at Herisau,
12km (7 miles) from
St Gallen, which opened on
3 October 1910.
The postcard was produced
to celebrate its opening.*

Herisau, neuer Bahnhof

VBZ Class Be4/4 No 1532, built by Schlieren between 1949 and 1952, plus trailer are on service 3 running between Zürich Hauptbahnhof and Klusplatz on 22 June 1958.

VBZ Class Be2/2 No 1244, supplied by Schlieren in 1912, plus trailer on service 6 between Zürich Hauptbahnhof and the zoo on 22 June 1958.

home of Germany's airships, designed by Count Ferdinand von Zeppelin. It is understood that in 1853/54, 3,000 tons of British bridge rail was supplied to Switzerland for use between St Gallen-Sargans and Walenstadt. It was replaced in 1863, but apparently can still be seen in use as fence posts in Domleschg and St Gallen. The Great Western Railway used its redundant bridge rail for the same purpose.

VERKEHRSBETRIEBE DER STADT ZÜRICH (VBZ)

VBZ horse trams started running in Zürich on 5 September 1882 using standard gauge; this system closed on 30 September 1900. A metre-gauge municipal tramway system, opened on 8 March 1894, was operated by electricity from the start at 600V dc. The total length of the system in the 1980s was about 64km (40 miles), but the system has been extended since that time.

VBZ Class Be4/4
No 1308 plus two trailers
are on service 7 on 22 June
1958. This was a cross-town
route to Seebach north of
the city.

VBZ Class Ce2/2 No 1,
built originally circa 1897,
of the Zürich-Oerlikon-
Seebach Tramway (ZOS).
It was restored between 1977
and 1986 by the Zürich
Tram Museum. The restored
tram is seen here approaching
Tiefenbrunnen whilst
participating in a special
museum car service on
23 September 1990.
Michael J. Russell

This commercial postcard dating from the early 20th century shows the wonderful façade of Basel SBB station. The station as shown here was opened on 24 June 1907 and replaced an older station on the site. Also illustrated is the tramway terminus in front of the station.

Basel station on 17 May 1952. In the foreground is Deutsche Bahn personenzugtenderlokomotive — 'tender' in German means 'tank' in English — Class 75 2-6-2T No 243. This class of locomotive was first introduced in 1900 and built by Maffei for the Badische Staatsbahn; a further batch was supplied to DB in 1923. Under the Third Reich, German railways became DR, reverting to DB in the west after 1945. There is plenty of Swiss rolling stock in the picture; the author was taking the train in the background, which was bound for the Austrian border and was hauled by an SBB Class Ae4/7.

Basler Verkehrsbetriebe (BVB) was the second largest tramway network in Switzerland at its peak. Here four-wheel tram No 95 and four-wheel trailer No 1125 are seen on route No 7 (Markplatz-Barfüsserplatz-Aeschenplatz-Bahnhof SBB-Binningen) on 17 May 1952, passing Elisabethen-Anlage (Gardens) and the Strasbourg Monument (designed by Bartholdi and presented to the city in commemoration of the aid given by the Swiss to the people of Strasbourg during the Franco-Prussian War of 1870).

BASEL: THE HUB OF CONTINENTAL TRAVEL

Too often this beautiful city is neglected by travellers who are hurrying through to some distant destination.

SCHWEIZERISCHE ALPENPOSTEN (PTT)

A postcard issued in 1923, showing a postbus in one of the alpine passes.
Biregg Verlag AG, CH–6003, Luzern

The Swiss Post Office started running bus services in 1906; the first route was between Bern and Detligen. Buses not only run regular services, which normally connect with the railway network, but they can also be hired for special excursions. They specialise in taking passengers through the alpine passes, weather conditions permitting, of course. The vehicles have the right of way on the roads as the author found out when driving in Switzerland. The drivers come up behind you and sound a very loud horn and, as soon as it is practical, one gets out of the way. The postbus service celebrated its centenary in 2006, when many preserved vehicles took part in a parade. This was similar to the parade organised by the author to mark the centenary of Great Western Railway omnibus services, which had commenced on 17 August 1903. A collection of preserved buses ran between Helston and the Lizard on 17 August 2003 celebrating the first route. The SBB celebrated the PTT centenary by giving locomotive No 460 006-0 a special livery in 2006.

A PTT Autobus — a Saurer Arbon Suisse, built circa 1955 (Reg No 2237) — on service 763 from St Moritz to Chur via the Julier Pass-Tiefencastel and Lenzerheide/Lai at St Moritz station on 3 June 1956.

Facsimile of an official PTT Autobus brochure.
PTT

A second PTT Autobus — Saurer Arbon Suisse, again built circa 1955 (Reg No 21518) — operates on service 775 from St Moritz to Castasegna via Maloja. The bus is seen at Sils/Segl Maria post office on 4 June 1956. Note the postbus symbol over the doorway; 50 years of service was being celebrated during 1956.

APPENDICES

SCHWEIZERISCHEN BUNDESBAHNEN (SBB)

Classification System — 1947

DAMPFLOKOMOTIVEN/STEAM LOCOMOTIVES

A	Tender locomotives over 80km/h
B	Tender locomotives 70-80 km/h
C	Tender locomotives 60-65 km/h
Ea	Tank locomotives over 80km/h
Eb	Tank locomotives 70-80km/h
Ec	Tank locomotives 60-65km/h
Ed	Tank locomotives 45-55km/h
E	Tank locomotives for secondary lines and shunting

British	Swiss	
OOO	0-6-0	3/3
oOOO	2-6-0 Mogul	3/4
OO	0-4-0	2/2
oOO	2-4-0	2/3
ooOO	4-4-0	2/4
oOOOO	2-8-0 Consolidation	4/5
OOO OOO	0-6-0+0-6-0 Mallet	3/3+3/3
oOOO OOO	2-6-0+0-6-0 Mallet	3/4+3/3
ooOOO	4-6-0	3/5
oOOOo	2-6-2 Prairie	3/5
oOOOOO	2-10-0 Decapod	5/6
ooOOO	4-8-0	4/6
ooOOOOo	4-8-2	4/7
ooOOOoo	4-6-4	3/7
ooOOOo	4-6-2 Pacific	3/6
oOOOoo	2-6-4	3/6
oOOOOo	2-8-2 Mikado	4/6

Examples:
3/3 = 3 axles with 3 driven
3/4 = 4 axles with 3 driven
5/6 = 6 axles with 5 driven
3/6 = 6 axles with 3 driven

ELEKTRISCHE LOKOMOTIVEN/ELECTRIC
LOCOMOTIVES

Re	Locomotives over 110km/h
Ae	Locomotives over 80km/h
Be	Locomotives 70-80km/h
Ce	Locomotives 60-65km/h
De	Locomotives 45-55km/h
Ee	Locomotives for secondary lines and shunting

TRAKTOREN/TRACTORS

Ta	Battery
Te	Electric
Tea	Electric/Battery
Tm	Diesel

TRIEBWAGEN/RAILCARS

Ce, CFm	Passenger railcars 110km/h
Fe, Fm	Luggage railcars 110km/h
RBe, RCm	Express railcars over 110km/h
Bt, BCt, CFt	Driving Trailer 110km/h

PERSONENWAGEN/PASSENGER COACHES

B	2nd Class
BC	2nd and 3rd Class
C	3rd Class
CF	3rd Class/Luggage

Classification System — Present Times All Lines

LOKOMOTIVEN/LOCOMOTIVES;
TRIEBWAGEN/RAILCARS

FIRST LETTER

R	Over 110km/h
A	85-110km/h
B	70-80km/h
C	60-65km/h
D	45-55km/h
E	Shunter
G	Narrow gauge
H	Rack; also rack and adhesion
T	Tractor
X	Departmental

SECOND LETTER

a	Battery
e	Electric
em	Electric and diesel
h	Rack railcars, when this letter precedes the 'a', 'e' or 'm' it is rack only; if it follows, then it is rack and adhesion

PERSONENWAGEN/PASSENGER COACHES

A	1st Class
B	2nd Class
D	Luggage
S	Saloon
Z	Post Office Van (PTT)

Examples — Locomotives, Trailers, etc:

Re4/4	Electric locomotive with 4 axles, all powered (Bo-Bo). Some of this class have been modified and have suffixes using Roman numerals (eg Re4/4^I or Re4/4^{II} etc.)
Ae6/6	Electric locomotive with 6 axles, all powered (Co-Co)
Be4/6	Electric locomotive with 6 axles, 4 powered
HGe2/2	Narrow-gauge electric locomotive with 2 axles, all powered
ABDe4/4	Electric railcar (Bo-Bo) with 1st, 2nd and luggage compartment

At the present time the numbering system is being changed to a computer system that will retain the letters but not the fractions. The Union Internationale des Chemins der Fer (UIC) has also devised a scheme for the complete renumbering of all railway vehicles throughout Europe. It is very complicated but it will show a country code, which for Switzerland will be 85, the type of vehicle and its own number. For example, Rc460 110 will become 91 85 8 460 110-0 CH (I hope!). For full information, consult *EUR2 European Railways Combined Volume II, 2010 Edition, Austria & Switzerland*, published by AEB Rail Publications (http://www.aebrail.co.uk)

Reisezugwagen der Schweizerischen Bundesbahnen

Carriages of the Swiss Federal Railways

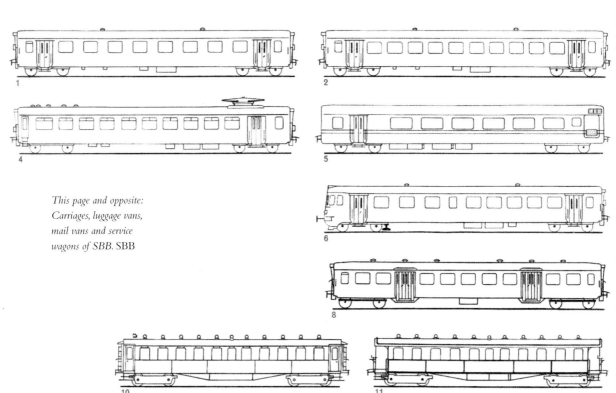

This page and opposite:
Carriages, luggage vans,
mail vans and service
wagons of SBB. SBB

Gepäck-, Post- und Dienstwagen der Schweizerischen Bundesbahnen

Luggage-, mail- and service wagons of the Swiss Federal Railways

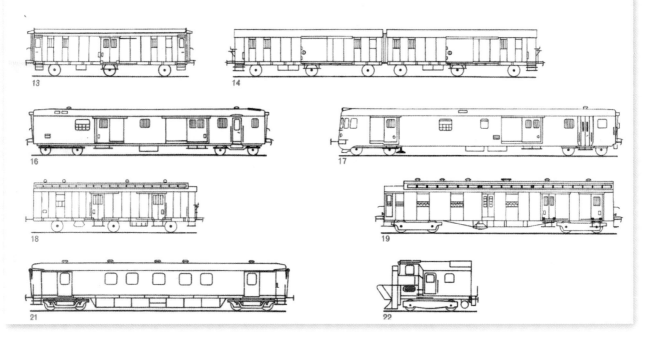

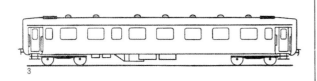

3

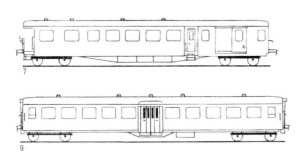

7

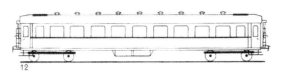

9

Nr. No	Serie Class	Wagen Nr. Series	Sitzplätze Seats	Anzahl Number	
1	A	2301..2560	48	180	Einheitswagen I. Klasse Standard carriage 1st class
2	B	6001..7040	80	766	Einheitswagen II. Klasse Standard carriage 2nd class
3	A RIC	2081—2100	42	20	RIC-Wagen, I. und II. Klasse RIC-carriage 1st and 2nd class
	B + Bc RIC	5121—5200	72	60	
4	WR	10101—10136	52	36	Speisewagen/Restaurant car
5	As	2801, 2802	36	2	Aussichtswagen Observation car
6	ABt	1961—1965	69	5	Steuerwagen/Control trailer
	ABt	1701—1720	56	20	Steuerwagen/Control trailer
	ABt	1721—1742	58	22	Steuerwagen/Control trailer
7	ABDi	4651—4655	48	5	I.-/II.-Klasswagen mit Gepäckabteil/Carriage 1st and 2nd class with luggage room Laderaum 14 m² Luggage room 14 m²
8	A	2201..2775	42—48	155	Leichtstahlwagen Light-steel carriage
	AB	3701—3810	55	110	Leichtstahlwagen Light-steel carriage
	B	5300..5726	72	420	Leichtstahlwagen Light-steel carriage
9	B	5751—5960	80	210	Leichtstahlwagen Light-steel carriage
10	A	2001..2967	42—62	28	Personenwagen I. Klasse Carriage 1st class
	AB	4101..4354	58—63	109	Personenwagen I. und II. Klasse Carriage 1st and 2nd class
	B	7050..9980	62—80	462	Personenwagen II. Klasse Carriage 2nd class
11	Ai	2901, 2902	48	2	Personenwagen I. Klasse Carriage 1st class
	ABi	4401..4602	56—70	79	Personenwagen I. und II. Klasse Carriage 1st and 2nd class
	Bi	7701..7902	64—80	78	Personenwagen II. Klasse Carriage 2nd class
12	A RIC	2022—2074	42	53	Personenwagen I. Klasse Carriage 1st class
	AB RIC	3601—3665	56	65	Personenwagen I. und II. Klasse Carriage 1st and 2nd class
	B RIC	5101..9960	72—78	238	Personenwagen II. Klasse Carriage 2nd class

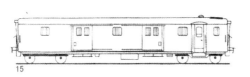

12

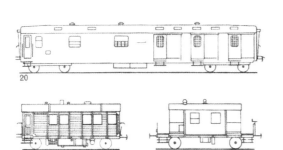

15

20

23   24

Nr. No	Serie Class	Wagen Nr. Series	Lastgrenze Load limit	Anzahl Number	
13	D3	18201..18470	8 t	204	Gepäckwagen Luggage van
14	D3-D3	18001—18013	2 × 8 t	13	Gepäckwagen Luggage van
15	D	18850—18999	12 t	150	Gepäckwagen Luggage van
16	DZ	19151—19160	12 t	10	Gepäckpostwagen Luggage and mail van
	Dt, DZt	1991—1995	12 t	5	Gepäck-Post-Steuer-wagen Luggage and mail control trailer
17	DZt	1901—1906	12 t	6	Gepäck-Post-Steuer-wagen Luggage and mail control trailer
18	Z3i; o; p; k	171..704	7,5—10,2 t	66	Postwagen/Mail van
19	Z; o	801..806	7,2—12 t	6	Postwagen/Mail van
20	Zi	401..1030	7—12 t	231	Postwagen/Mail van
21	X	90310..90339	16—19 t	18	Dienstwagen Service wagon
22	Xrot. e	99	Tara 30 t Tare 30 t	1	Schneeschleuder Snow-plough
23	X 2	90101—90110	Dienstgew. 23 t In working order 23 t	10	Heizwagen Heating wagon
24	Db	10311..10440	Dienstgew. 10 t In working order 10 t	125	Dienstbegleitwagen Service wagon

PRESERVED STEAM LOCOMOTIVES

*SBB Class A3/5 No 705,
built SLM in 1904,
Wks.No.1550, shown here
on the roundhouse turntable
at Delémont in July 1997.
Delémont lies between Basel
and Biel/Bienne. In
connection with the 150 years
celebration of the SBB
No 705 worked a special
train from Delémont to
Glovelier. C. E.Vier*

*SBB Class B3/4 No 1367
was built by SLM in 1916
(Works No 2557);
it is seen here in 2011 at
Rothrist whilst working an
SBB Historic service from
Brugg to Langnau via
Luzern.* Bryan Stone

SBB Class C5/6 No 2969, which was built by SLM in 1916 (Works No 2522) was for a while at Sargan, illustrated here, heating oil tank wagons, at the former roundhouse, before going back to Erstfeld and then, after withdrawal, being 'plinthed' in Winterthur. This is the engine to be put back in service by Eurovapor in Sulgen, and its chassis was long in Interlaken in the Ballenberg workshop. Reunion, in Sulgen, of chassis and boiler are at the time of writing imminent.
Bryan Stone

SBB Class E3/3 No 8512, built by SLM in 1911 (Works No 2135), is one of a number of this class of 0-6-0WT to survive in preservation. It is part of the VHS collection and was recorded on an occasion when the VHS Vallorbe collection was being aired.
Mario Stefani via Bryan Stone

TYPES OF RACK SYSTEMS USED IN SWITZERLAND

1. The ladder rack of Niklaus Riggenbach (see description on page 148).

2. The double brackar system of Dr Roman Abt. Although published in 1884, it was not used until 1890, its first application being on the Monte Generoso Railway. The rack consisted of flat-toothed plates, of which two or three (according to the tractive power) were bolted together on chairs in such a way that the tooth of one plate in regard to the other was displaced by half or one-third of the pitch. This pitch amounts to 12cm (4.7in). The Abt system of rack ensured a quiet motion of gearing, allowing trains to work at higher speeds. It was especially applicable to long railways on the mixed system. The Abt rack is the most used of all the systems and, *circa* 1911, about 520km (323) miles were fitted with it. In the earlier years of the 20th century it was constructed by the Union Dortmund and by Cammell Laird & Co of Sheffield.

3. The taper head rack bar of Emil Strub, which used a broad-footed toothed rail having a wedge-formed top, similar to the rail used on rope railways, provided with clamp brake-gear. This head of the rack furnishes a good guide for the safety grips; the latter, however, proved to be unsatisfactory when worked as brakes. Strub's rack-gear was first put into use in 1898 on the Jungfraubahn. The pitch is generally 10cm (3.94in). The Bern foundry of Ludwig von Roll had taken over its construction.

4. The double gear-rack bar with horizontal gear-wheels for ultra-steep gradients, devised in 1886 by Colonel Edouard Locher for the Pilatus Railway. The wheels do not need any flanges because the centre rack rail holds the train in position. It was first used in 1888 on the Pilatus Railway, which has a maximum gradient of 1 in 2.08. The arrangement consists of a plate having gear-teeth on each side of it, into which two gear-wheels drive, placed opposite to each other; these rack-plates, being riveted to a Vautrin rail, which is so rolled that guide-discs can be provided on the gear-wheel, ensure a correct guiding of the vehicle and prevent riding of the wheels. The pitch is 8.6cm (3.37in). The heavy gradient necessitates a road very solidly built in masonry, the whole being properly anchored down.

5. A variation to the Riggenbach ladder-rack was designed by Mr Klose (of semi-articulated locomotive fame) for the St Gallen-Gais Railway.

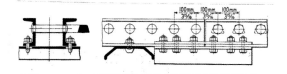

1 Rack rail system by Niklaus Riggenbach (1817-1899).

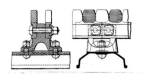

2 Double rack bar system by Dr. Roman Abt (1850-1933).

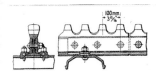

3 Taper head rack bar system by Emile Strub (1858-1909).

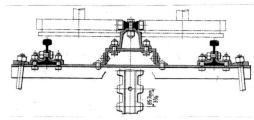

4 The special rack bar with horizontal teeth on each side by Eduard Locher-Freuler (1840-1910).

There are four types of rack systems in use in Switzerland.
Railway Gazette

BIBLIOGRAPHY

100 Jahre bernische Eisenbahnpolitik/50 Jahre Lötschberg Bahn; R. Bratschi; BLS; undated

Beiträge zur Schweizerischen Eisenbahngeschichte; Ernst Mathys; Kümmerly & Frey; 1954

Die Brünigbahn; J. Hardmeyer; Druck und Orell Füssli & Co; 1888

Der Dampfbetrieb Der Schweizerischen Eisenbahnen 1847-1922; Alfred Moser (Locomotivführer der SBB, Basel); 1923

Die Drahtseilbahn, Territet-Montreux-Glion; Emil Strub; H. R. Sauerländer; 1888

Der Grosse Duden Bildwörterbuch; Illustrated Technical German Dictionary; Bibliographisches Institut; 1958

Die elektrischen und Dieseltriebfahrzeuge Schweizerischer Eisenbahnen; Claude Jeanmaire; 1970

Ein Jahrhundert Schweizer Bahnen 1847-1947; Jubiläumswerk; 1957

Hundert Jahre Schweizerbahnen 1841-1941; Ernst Mathys; Bibliothekar SBB; 1943.

Industrial Locomotives of Switzerland; Richard Bowen; Industrial Railway Society; 1973

Lokomotiven und Triebwagen der Schweizer Bahnen; four volumes; Peter Willen; Orell Füssli; 1982 to1985

Mountain Rack Railways of Switzerland; J. R. Bardsley; Oakwood Press; 1999

Nos Locomotives; M. Hauri for SBB/CFF; Librairie Payot; 1946

Railway Electrification in Switzerland; H. Loosli; SBB; 1954

Railway Gazette; articles and special editions concerning Switzerland

Reise und Verkehrskarte der Schweiz; Map; Verlag A. Meissner/Kümmerly & Frey
  SBB CFF FFS; SBB; *circa* 1963

Schweiz Offizielle Strassenkarte; Touring-Club der Schweiz map; Kümmerly & Frey.

Schweizerischer Lokomotivbau 1871-1971; SLM Winterthur; 1971

Sea Breezes; magazine articles concerning lake steamers of Luzern

Swiss Express; magazine of the Swiss Railway Society

Swiss Motive Power Survey; C. W. Sex and B. J. Prigmore; Electric Railway Society; 1974

Swiss Mountain Railways: Volume 1 — Around Luzern and Interlaken; Philip J. Kelley and Donald Binns; Trackside Publications; 1999

Swiss Narrow Gauge featuring steam in the Alps; John Organ; Middleton Press; 2003

Swiss Railways Locomotives, Multiple Units & Trams; Third Edition; Platform 5; 2009

Swiss Railways/Chemins de fer Suisses — Locomotives & Railcars; First Edition; Platform 5; 1991

Switzerland's Amazing Railways; Cecil J. Allen; Thomas Nelson & Sons Ltd; 1953

The Essential Guide to Swiss Heritage and Tourist Railways; Mervyn Jones; Oakwood Press; 2007

Tramways and Light Railways of Switzerland and Austria; R. J. Buckley; Light Rail Transit Association; 1984

Unsere Triebfahrzeuge; Paul Winter; Orell Füssli; 1959

Various Guide books — Ward Lock, Blue Guide, Fodor, etc

Various issues of the official Swiss timetables

Verkehrshaus; (Luzern) Guide; 1987

Verzeichnis des Rollmaterials Triebfahrzeuge; Official Handbook; SBB; 1947

Zum Abschluss der Elektrifikation der SBB; SBB; *circa* 1960

Zürich-Baden die Wege der Schweizerischen Eisenbahnen; Oskar Welti; Orell Füssli; 1946

INDEX